D0889416

Jim Kachenmeister

Under the Tuscan Thumb

How "Building Dreams in Tuscany"
Turned into a Nightmare

Jim Kachenmeister

DEDICATION

To Martin Prince

Under the Tuscan Thumb

Contents

ACKNOWLEDGMENTS

A big thank-you to those who read all or part of the early drafts of this book and who have given me wonderful advice along the way. Thanks to Jeff Harding and Jane Cotter, Susan Murphy, Chris Howell, Cherryl Kachenmeister and Tom Berthiaume. I am especially grateful to The Prince, for his wise counsel.

To my wonderful editor, Fiona Cameron Lister, and her team at Twinclian Press, thank you not only for your literary skills, but also for your personal coaching, which brought out the essential elements in the story that were hiding inside.

Finally, to Debbie, the more accomplished author in the family, thank you most for your understanding of the importance of my sharing this somewhat painful tale with the world.

Prologue

As I left the *notaio's* office in the historic center of Lucca, I had never felt more alone. This was supposed to be a day to celebrate. In 2007, I bought a centuries-old ruin, Il Borghetto in San Gennaro, with high hopes of *Building Dreams in Tuscany* for others. I had fought through the bureaucracy of the *permesso* process for two years. Our Sicilian builder, Nicola Padrino, had built a masterpiece using the stones and bricks from the original ruin, with artisan touches that would live on for centuries to come. To find the money to finish the construction I had gone against the advice of people wiser than me and had sold our home in London. Seven years after starting this venture, I had just sold five of the six apartments. So why did I feel like crying?

The reality was that not a single euro from these sales went into my bank account and only one owner wanted to keep his apartment. My great friend and mentor in the UK, Martin Prince, had bought several of the apartments as a favor and to protect his initial investment as the dark days swallowed me up. He wanted to sell them as soon as I could find buyers.

I had no prospects to sell any of his apartments. Il Borghetto was a beautiful asset, sitting there generating no revenue, draining money from my dwindling bank account to pay for the interest, maintenance and taxes until I came up with a solution.

I also owned a second project in Arsina, a spectacular piece of land in the hills overlooking Lucca four miles outside the walls, where I had more than €1,000,000 invested. My permission to build five more homes there, good for only five years, had just expired. As things spiraled out of control, it became harder to face my wife, Debbie, and tell her the cold truth. The voice in my head that I woke up to every morning was brutal in its assessment. "You've cashed in your pension by selling your home in London, have nothing to show for it, and have totally screwed up your retirement." How could this have gone so horribly wrong? As alone as I felt in that moment, walking up the cobblestone street of the Via Fillungo in Lucca, I thought back to the day in 2007 when three of us started this venture with laughter and high hopes.

Chapter 1 -- "Build It and They Will Come"

What a great line. It was the favorite expression of Lou Codardo, a Canadian who was born in Italy, moved to Toronto when he was five, and who returned to Lucca after retiring from the advertising business. He had made some big profits here, buying up old barns from the local farmers and building homes for foreign buyers. He sold one of his homes to an American couple and he supervised the construction of another big home, which he sold to a German doctor. One of the outbuildings on the German's property was turned into a beautiful small home and sold to a lovely Irish restaurateur and his family. Everything Lou touched seemed to turn to gold.

When you look back on the property market in Tuscany between 2000 and 2007, the only negative factor was that other areas of Italy, thanks to the influx of low-cost airlines, were starting to boom as well, because Tuscany was so expensive. If real estate is about "location, location, location," there was no better place to be than in the heart of Tuscany. Sting owned a villa here, as did Elton John. Everybody wanted to live in *bella Toscana*.

So in the spring of 2007, when Lou approached me and another friend to sound us out on starting a property development company, I was ready to listen. Two years into retirement, I was a little bored, missing the power and the buzz of corporate life. Lou's proposal was to start a company funded partly by us but the primary money would flow from a colleague of his in Toronto, who was an investor with connections. We would simply extend the strategy that Lou had used so successfully, one house at a time, to include multiple projects. We would buy dilapidated farmhouses and barns, convert them into holiday homes, and sell them to the hordes of foreigners who also wanted a piece of paradise under the Tuscan sun. With enough investor money, we could have four or five projects on the go at any one time. Lou already had the first project lined up: il Borghetto in San Gennaro, a centuries-old ruin that could be turned into six apartments with a projected 40% return on our investment. My buy-in to being one of three partners in this venture was less than 10% of my net worth. It seemed like a risk well worth taking. Let the fun begin!

The fun began immediately as I took on the challenge of creating a name for our new venture. "Well, since we know our wives are the real CEOs in our lives," I joked, "why not name it after them?"

Twenty minutes later I came up with Anderó Srl (Srl being the designation for a limited company in Italy). The "An" came from Lou's wife, Anne. The "de" from my wife, Debbie. And the "ro" from Rosemary, our third partner's wife. And with an accent on the final "ó", our name had the added benefit of being the old-fashioned way to say, "I will go!" in Italian. Brilliant. *Avanti!* Onward! Let's get our building permit for il Borghetto and get started!

Not so fast. As I came to learn the hard way, the term *permesso* (permission, or in the case of a house, a building permit) should sound the alarm bells for anyone who is about to take on the red tape of Italy.

Italy is well known for its bureaucracy, but there is one aspect of it that is both a curse and a blessing, and that is the protection of Italian architecture and the control over what and where you can build. Nowhere in Italy is this more evident than in the hills of Tuscany. With very few exceptions, you cannot build a house in the hills unless a building already exists on that spot. If you have a barn and you want to turn it into a house – fine. You will be allowed the same number of square meters as is the size of the barn; the architecture when you are finished will be in keeping with what the barn looked like; and you will re-use the materials from the barn as much as possible.

You cannot build a California ranch-style home in Tuscany. You will have a red terra cotta tile roof, some stucco and stone, and you will only be able to paint the house a color from a narrow range of acceptable Tuscan pastels. These laws have served a great purpose and for anyone who has driven through Tuscany and admired the hill towns and the sparse number of homes scattered in the hillsides, it is the bureaucracy and the tight building regulations keeping it this way. I shudder to think what an American developer might do to this beautiful countryside if these rules didn't exist. Fifty-unit apartment complexes spread across the hillsides would be common, I'm sure. We have none of that here.

While avoiding taxes might be Italy's favorite sport, getting around the bureaucracy is their second favorite. Almost every Italian has done something to their home or property that is technically illegal, and Debbie and I had our own personal experience with this when we bought our house in 2004. It was still under construction when we bought it, and it was missing a few key features that we wanted. So our builder filed the variance to put in two more windows, two fireplaces and the *forno*, the outdoor wood-burning oven. There were proper drawings to show where everything was going to go, with precise dimensions. The *forno* was designed to go up against the outside of our house. I paid no attention to the positioning; I was happy enough that they approved these five exceptions.

When our friend, Doug, a former graphic designer and one with *un buon occhio*, a good eye, saw the plans he said, "This is going to look awful up against your house. It's too big. You have a great spot for it over there across your garden, fifteen meters from your house." He was absolutely right, and after we got our permission, we built it where Doug suggested.

At this point, one of two things could have happened. If the inspector came out after we installed the *forno* and saw it in the wrong location, he could have made us tear it down. Our builder and the architect told us, "They won't come out to inspect something as minor as that." So we took a chance.

Here's the part of the game I like best. If you aren't caught in five years and it is a minor transgression, most of the time it will be overlooked and perhaps a small fine will be assessed when you sell the house. I now boldly confess to my sin, knowing that more than five years have passed since we built our *forno* fifteen meters from its designated spot.

Our personal experience was nothing compared to what we were about to go through with our Anderò properties. Even when you do everything right and you have a proper building plan adhering to all the rules, it can take between eighteen months and two years to get approval. The mountain of paperwork is staggering. Lou and I had regular meetings about il Borghetto with our *geometra* (the designer and the one who shepherds your plans through the red tape) at which we had to sign a pile of documents a foot high. There were schematics of everything, from every angle, for the dozens of technocrats to peruse.

We had to satisfy two groups to get our

building permit and they love to tinker with each other's decisions. The *Comune* (town council) is the first group we had to satisfy. After our submission had aged for the appropriate number of months in the *Comune*, they finally got around to commenting on the design and recommending changes. Then they sent it off to the *Belle Arte* (the arts council) where the fun really begins. Their job is to make sure the design and building materials are in keeping with the traditions of the area where you are building. Their real function is to make work for themselves and annoy the *Comune*.

We submitted a beautiful design for an all-stone building, in keeping with the centuries-old ruin that we bought. We followed all the rules. No problem with the *Comune*.

The *Belle Arte* didn't like it.

Il Borghetto was a magnificent structure with an exterior of 100% stone. For some unknown reason, the *Belle Arte* wanted it to be rebuilt with stone at both ends, and the rest of the building would have traditional stucco walls. Why? We will never know. One of their other specialties is to change your windows and doors. We had designed three beautiful arched doorframes outside our three ground floor apartments. The *Belle Arte* turned the middle one into a square frame. I would bet anything that if we had designed square frames, they would have changed them to arches. It's all job security for them. Changes mean more paperwork and a guarantee of more weeks and months to approve your changes when the drawings come back through their office a second time.

The *Belle Arte* had our plans for months the first time. We tried to squeeze our *geometra* to put some pressure on them to complete their assessment and return the documents to the *Comune*. He shrugged and told us, "We should hear back from them by the end of the month." He never said which month. Lou was a casual acquaintance of a local politician and one day we heard that his wife worked in the *Belle Arte*. Lou and I invited him for a coffee and we told him our tale of woe. Within a couple of weeks, the *Belle Arte* released our project. Italy runs on personal relationships and one of ours finally brought us a little joy. But not for long.

When the *Belle Arte* was through tweaking our design, it went back to the *Comune* for their approval. Gee, what could go wrong with this process? Sure enough, our documents bounced back and forth between the two agencies for many more months and we never knew quite what the disagreements were.

The *Belle Arte* is also notorious for making you put in a minimalist swimming pool. "One meter of terracotta around the pool, then grass," is their most common decision, wanting to keep the area around the pool as natural as possible. Want to put down some permanent flagstones in your garden and have a pergola with wisteria growing over it for shade? That needs separate approval from the *Comune* and *Belle Arte* and good luck getting an answer in less than a year.

A benefit of all this bureaucracy and nitpicking

is that it pretty much guarantees that there will never be an oversupply of property in the Tuscan hills. You never have to worry about someone building next to your house and spoiling your view. If there is not an existing structure there, no one will be allowed to build a home.

il Cubano

The third member of our newly formed Anderó Srl was a charming Cuban-American, Raul, whom we call *il Cubano*. His family fled Cuba when he was a young man, shortly after Castro came to power and confiscated the family sugar cane plantation. After getting his undergraduate degree in engineering in Havana, *il Cubano* arrived in the US and earned an MBA at NYU and then embarked on a career that took him to South Africa, Brazil, the Philippines and Singapore. He did everything from helping to build the World Trade Center in New York City, to attending parties with Ferdinand and Imelda Marcos. He had just sold his engineering firm in Miami to move to Lucca. He bought a ruin high in the hills and had his own adventure building a spectacular home. Halfway through his project he was shut down for some minor building violations, anonymously reported by some neighbors who preferred to keep that particular mountaintop pristine. It all came good in the end, but he lost about eighteen months in the process, fighting to get his building permit restored.

After the first year of Anderò, when Lou was still talking about taking on more risk and more projects even though investors were hard to find, *il Cubano* asked to be bought out. We turned to Lou's investor friend in Canada, Kevin the Rainmaker, and to his credit, he bought out *il Cubano's* shares. This was strictly an investment for Kevin, and he was happy to let Lou and I run the business, as we were full time residents of Lucca. The three-man company responsible for *Building Dreams in Tuscany* was now down to the two of us.

With the beautiful ruin that was to become il Borghetto safely in our portfolio, Lou quickly went for the close on Project Arsina with the farmer he had been talking to for the past six

months. We quickly named it la Porcellaia –
The Pig Farm

La Porcellaia in Arsina

High in hills of Arsina, near a smattering of
farm houses, villas and olive groves four miles
outside the walls of Lucca, stood a monstrosity
of a big, abandoned, cinder block building.
How in the world anyone received permission
to build a pig farm on this hillside, with
spectacular views looking south over Lucca, is
beyond me. They were the luckiest pigs in the
world; well, for every day except one, that is.
The building was complete with electricity,
water, and two large rooms with feeding
troughs. Eight hundred square meters (8600
square feet) of luxury porcine living quarters
with views to die for... literally. It had been
abandoned years earlier and as you can't build
in the hills of Tuscany unless there is already a
structure there, it was the volume of buildable
square meters that we were buying.

Our can't-miss formula in those heady days of
2007 was this: buy a property for 1,000 euros

(about $1,350 at that time) per square meter of buildable housing. Spend another 2,000 euros per square meter to build it, which was enough to include the pool and landscaping. We were going to build these homes in eighteen months and sell them for 4,500 to 5,000 euros per square meter. La Porcellaia was another project with a supposed 40% return on our investment, just like il Borghetto. If only Kevin the Rainmaker could come through with a couple more million in additional financing, we could put some money down on a third and fourth project. *Avanti* Anderò!

We were all a bit giddy with excitement for our new venture. We spent the weeks after forming Anderò touring Tuscany looking at everything from barns that were falling down to huge villas with multiple outbuildings, just waiting to be turned into luxury resort hotels and spas.

In late 2007, I was naively optimistic about the future of Anderò. The application for our building permit for il Borghetto had just been sent off to the *Comune* with our *geometra* telling us, "six months, and then we can start construction", the first of many lies from him. We had closed on our second project, la Porcellaia. We started spending money on marketing both projects, hoping to sell one or two of the apartments before construction began, just from the beautiful drawings. I was calm and happy.

I didn't ask myself what could go wrong. Build it and they will come! Lou's mantra made him the Pied Piper of Lucca, and I happily followed along. This was going to be fun, easy and profitable. A few people had raised their eyebrows when I mentioned I was going into business with Lou, but if he was a good businessman and we were going to get rich together, I could overlook a few character flaws.

All I could think of was that the name I came up with, *Anderó Srl* – was brilliant! As was my marketing tag line: *Building Dreams in Tuscany*. We weren't just building holiday homes. We were helping people realize the same dream all of us had found by moving outside this historic walled city of Lucca, in the heart of one of the most desired regions in the world, Tuscany.   The reasonable amount of money I was putting into Anderò didn't worry me. Embracing risk was something I was used to. I had done so time and again in my business career. The risk of starting up Anderò seemed minor compared to our decision to leave our careers behind in London two years earlier to live in this beautiful paradise. Now <u>that</u> was a risk.

Chapter 2 -- Let's Move to Italy

"Let's quit our jobs and move to Italy." I dropped this on Debbie one night after work in the late autumn of 2004, giving the glass of wine I had poured her a bit of time to take the edge off another busy day at school. I had been mulling this over in my mind for a couple of months. I'm sure I was on my second gin and tonic when it came tumbling out.

We were blessed to be two Americans, and Brits as well, having recently attained British citizenship, enjoying all that life had to offer in London. With two great jobs, we relished going to the theater, walking on the Hampstead Heath, eating at our favorite Indian restaurants, and soaking up the culture and the buzz that is London.

In 1988, during our first stint in London, we had reluctantly moved back to the US three weeks after our wedding when I received a promotion too good to turn down. It was a painful move. We had arrived just a year apart a few years earlier. We met and fell in love - with each other and with London simultaneously. We fought to return here during our seven years back in America. For us, London is one of the most vibrant and exciting cities on earth and our pledge to each other had been that once we moved there the second time, we were never going to leave.

We got our second chance in 1995 when Debbie was offered a great position as the Primary and Middle School Principal at a prestigious international school in Kensington, and Kodak, my employer at the time, graciously found a European role for me as well. But now, after nine years back in London, the rose-colored glasses had taken on a slightly different tint for me. London's infrastructure problems and high cost of living are the price of admission for living there. A creaky Underground, a stressed National Health Service, and the highest per-passenger rail fares of any country in Europe were only some of England's woes. Spending the equivalent of $100 for the pleasure of High Tea at The Ritz or at Brown's Hotel always took a little of the joy away from those special times for me.

My "Let's quit our jobs and move to Italy," surprise wasn't out of the blue. I was feeling a bit stale in my job. We had just purchased a holiday home outside of Lucca after having spent many summer vacations in this beautiful part of Tuscany. I had done my analysis showing how much less it would cost to live in Lucca compared to London. More importantly, we were both in love with Lucca.

Our first exposure to this relatively

undiscovered city between Pisa and Florence
was in 2000, when we went to our friends'
wedding. Doug and Doris left their successful
careers in advertising in Minneapolis to live
their dream in Tuscany. They bought a derelict
mill house oozing with charm, historical
significance, and no two windows the same
size. They were lovingly and painfully
restoring it to run as a vacation rental.

My cousin, Cherryl, and her husband, Tom,
flew over from the States and Tom and I had a
memorable week in a cooking school near
Arezzo the week prior to the wedding. We
were in the kitchen for six hours a day making
traditional pasta dishes, plus *risotto; gnocchi;*
the delicious peasant soup, *ribollita;* the famous
four-inch thick *bistecca di Fiorentina;* Italian
vegetable flans, *sformati;* and *pizza.* Every
meal included a *dolce,* such as *torta di mandorle e
cioccolato* (flourless chocolate almond cake) or
cantucci, (almond biscuits) dipped in *Vin Santo,*
the delicious dessert wine. We celebrated our
culinary skills by feasting on all that we had
made at lunch and dinner, helped along by

generous amounts of *Chianti Classico* under the perfect summer sky. My already great love for Italian cuisine climbed steadily up the scale with each passing day.

Our instructor was a great chef, a Sicilian named Giuseppe, who happened to live in London. The fifteen of us in the class bonded during the week and six of us who lived in London continued to get together to host monthly dinner parties long after the course was over.

Chef Giuseppe would break out a bottle of wine in the kitchen about fifteen minutes before lunch and dinner, as we moved out into the garden to feast on our creations. As the days went by, our *aperitivo* began to appear earlier each day.

The dishes and the menu-planning built to a grand banquet as we approached our last dinner together on the Thursday night of the course. *Bistecca di maiale* (pork) and *cannellini* beans, Tuscan staples, were on the menu and the red wine flowed. Speeches were made, a dozen toasts to Chef Giuseppe rang out, and newly formed friendships deepened. To say that we might have been over-served would be an understatement.

We were all due back in the kitchen at 9:30 the next morning for one last three-hour session, followed by lunch, and our departure; Tom and I for the rehearsal dinner for Doris and Doug's wedding. It was a sorry-ass group who stumbled into the kitchen that morning. Some people were clearly not going to make it until *pranzo*. Chef Giuseppe took one look at us and said, *"Forse un po' di vino?"* Perhaps a little wine?

You've never seen so many grateful faces. Hangovers disappeared in the next thirty minutes and by 10:00 a.m. we were slicing and dicing, cooking in harmony again.

Doris and Doug's wedding was wonderful. After the ceremony in the Town Hall of Montecatini, a famous spa town thirty minutes from Lucca, we all took the *funicolare* (a cog railway), up to Montecatini Alto, an idyllic village on the top of a mountain, where the reception and dinner spilled out into the central *piazza* on a perfect June summer evening.

Our week in a farmhouse in the hills outside Lucca after the wedding was spent lounging by the pool, trying out our new culinary skills, and exploring Lucca. The next summer we rented the same farmhouse for two weeks instead of one and had friends join us for one of the weeks. The following year it was three weeks; and then four weeks a year later. By then our farmhouse felt like an extended home for us and in one of our delirious moments, enhanced by some *Limoncello* under the stars at midnight on a hot summer's night, we asked the owners if they would ever consider selling it. What were we thinking? By then we knew very well about the family traditions that are so important in Italian life.

Children in Italy, for the most part, don't grow up and move away from the family nest. It is common for parents to convert the old stone barn on their property to a proper home where the children can live when they are grown. We know several families where three generations are living in the same compound of two or three farmhouses. How wonderful for the grandchildren to have their *nonna* and *nonno* so close at hand. Much easier to do the *passeggiata* (a long family walk together, usually on top of the wall in Lucca) on Sunday afternoons after a leisurely family lunch. Alas, the owners of the villa, with three young children, had future plans for the renovated farmhouse next door to their villa, so our buying it was out of the question.

By the time we were doing our four-week rentals, we were inviting one or two couples at a time to spend a week with us. Then we traded them in for more cousins or friends from London for the next week. Perhaps a week just for the two of us might be thrown in there, but we had our happiest times sharing "our Tuscan summer holiday home" with friends and family. We only got it wrong once by somehow matching up our London minister and his wife, with Cherryl and Tom, who described himself as a "grumpy agnostic" when asked about his faith by the minister's wife.

After a few years, we knew that Lucca was a place we wanted to return to again and again. Low cost airlines had begun popping up in Europe, driving down the price of an airline ticket between London and Pisa from £500 to less than £100 in many instances. These budget carriers were setting up business in secondary airports throughout Europe by negotiating massive concessions to keep their operating costs low, in exchange for the economic surge of hundreds of thousands of new visitors each year to boost the local economy. Lucca is just forty minutes from both Pisa and Florence airports and with a flying time of just over two hours from London, it became easy to come down for long weekends and summer holidays.

Every time we took the two hour flight from Heathrow to Pisa, we were transported to *la bella vita* that everyone loves; fabulous scenery, warm, generous people who put up with our bad Italian with a smile, and the diet that keeps these people going until the Italian pension system can no longer cope. Italy has one of the longest life expectancy rates of any country in the world. The secret to this is well known; extra virgin olive oil, red wine, tomatoes, locally sourced meat, poultry and fish, all prepared simply and never served to excess. We never felt so healthy than after our holidays in Italy. Even the *gelato* is better for you than what passes for ice cream in most other countries.

So it was with more than a little giddy excitement that Debbie and I decided, after four years of renting, to start looking for a holiday home where we could spend four to six weeks each year and perhaps rent it out when we were not using it. We made an offer to buy a small rustic home near Doug and Doris, but as fate would have it, while the seller hesitated, we found our future home even closer to Lucca.

La Casa Gialla

Eighty percent complete when we first saw it,
it wasn't the barn-being-turned-into-a-house
that made us say "wow". It was the view.
Only four miles from Lucca, birthplace of
Puccini, high in the hills with views of the
Apennine and Apuane mountain ranges, we
found la Casa Gialla. The Yellow House. It
sounds better in Italian, like most things do.
One of our stores here is called *La Casa delle
Scarpe*. Say that a couple of times out loud.
Say it with some Italian enthusiasm,
pronouncing every syllable. Now doesn't that
sound better than "House of Shoes"?

We made an offer and it was accepted by the
lovely Giulio, who would become a friend and
an unfortunate business associate years later.
He was good for my Italian because he is a
chiacchierone, a chatterbox. If I asked him about
some detail of our house, I knew I was in for a
twenty-minute explanation. But he was
sincere and he genuinely wanted to make us
happy with our decision to buy the house; he
went all out to make sure we understood

everything he was doing. And as the owner of a custom kitchen business, he helped us design a beautiful *cucina*, complete with famous white *Carrara* marble from the mountains just 25 miles away; the same mountains where Michelangelo came to select the piece of marble that would become the David.

I flew to Pisa on September 11th, 2003 to sign the contracts. The extra security at Stansted airport was a bit suffocating -- they confiscated my tiny carry-on as everything had to go in the hold of the plane that day. It was the second anniversary of the 9/11 attacks and the UK was on high alert, as was the US. I was in Edinburgh on business on 9/11 two years earlier, and I'll never forget the outpouring of condolences I received in the days after from some of the normally gruff and gritty London east-enders in my company. As one of only a couple of Americans in a company of 650 employees, I was truly moved by how gutted they were for America and for me.

The house was eight months away from completion, so we were able to add some features that Giulio hadn't considered. With magnificent views to the east, his architect had planned only one window and a glass-fronted door facing that direction. When we proposed two more windows on either side of the front door, Giulio expressed his concern that we would be too hot in summer. When you've had these views all your life, I guess they aren't as special to the Italians as they are to those of us who swoon over them.

Italians don't use air-conditioning. The more windows you have, the harder it is to keep the house cool. They close all their windows that face the sun during the day in the summer, and let those two-feet thick walls keep the house cool. And it works. Giulio sighed and relented on the windows, no doubt saying, "*stranieri pazzi*," crazy foreigners.

We went to the *Comune* and the *Belle Arte* with our *variante*, the variance, for the two windows, two fireplaces and most importantly, our *forno*, styled to look like a miniature version of the house. After that week spent cooking in Arezzo before the wedding, I had to have my own pizza oven.

The following spring the house was finished and we flew down to Lucca to start furnishing it. Doris and Doug were kind enough to meet the delivery truck at la Casa Gialla before our arrival to take delivery of our bed so we could sleep there. We rushed around buying dishes, cutlery, linens, and all the other basics. We ordered a sofa bed that would be delivered a couple of months later.

We had excitedly invited Cherryl and Tom back over from the States to be our first guests at la Casa Gialla, even though Debbie and I were working hard up in London. They supervised the new sofa bed's arrival through a bedroom window when it wouldn't fit through the front door. They were having a great time inaugurating our new home without us.

Finally, it was too much for me. My other cousin, Pam, correctly predicted to Cherryl, "There's no way Jim and Debbie are going to let you be the first ones to stay in their new home without them being there." She was right. We were too excited to stay away, so we flew down for a long weekend to celebrate la Casa Gialla with some menu choices from Tom's and my cooking course. Debbie and Cherryl found the perfect *rustico* dining room table for us at the monthly antique market in Lucca, and we were off and running.

We spent our summer holiday there as well, putting the final touches on decorating our new holiday home. As we finished, I was having second thoughts about renting it out to vacationers when we weren't there, which was our original plan. How could Debbie and I sit there in London, with strangers in our home, worrying about the red wine stains they would no doubt be leaving on the *Carrara* marble? By the end of the year, I was dreaming of a life in *bella Italia.*

"Debbie, let's quit our jobs and move to la Casa Gialla."

I had it all figured out. The cost of living in Lucca was going to be 40% less than living in

London. Even though we were giving up our incomes, we had enough money saved and enough assets in real estate that even if our assets increased just 5% per year, we would spin off enough money to leave our principal retirement money intact and we could live off the increase in property values and gains in the stock market. Sure, there could be ups and downs, but on average, a 5% annual return was easily within reach based on the economy of the past 20 years.

Another element of my retirement strategy, which gave me great comfort, was that we had assets in three different countries, in three different currencies. Having worked in London as an ex-pat for an American company, I was paid in US dollars for all but the last five years of my career. So the bulk of our cash savings was in the US. We owned property in London and in Italy. We had assets in dollars…and British pounds…and euros. Fantastic. If there were ever a financial crisis with one currency, it would be to the benefit of another currency that we held. If things ever got too far out of whack, we could move assets from one country to another and take advantage of an exchange rate in our favor. "Clever boy," I thought.

Debbie is not as impulsive as I am so it took some time for her to process all this. "I'll miss my students, the parents, my colleagues," she said. Greatly respected as a teacher at an international school in North London, Debbie could see herself there for many years to come. But she is also an adventurer. "Are you sure?" she asked in the days after my proposal. "It's a big risk." It was a few weeks later, when her love of Tuscany, the lure of living in Lucca, and her confidence in me that I had the financial piece figured out, that she put her love of London aside to say, "Let's do it!"

It was time to plot my escape from the corporate world.

It is common practice in the UK to have notice periods for most positions. You don't quit your job in the UK. You give notice. The notice period for senior executives is typically long; in my case, one year. This is primarily driven by the fear that your chief executive is going to run off tomorrow and work for the competition. So if you walk in and give notice and your company thinks you are going to the competition, you are sent home on "garden leave". It's a lovely term. Time to work in your garden. How British! You are still employed and paid until the end of your notice period but you can't go off and work for anyone else. You are expected to stay home and tend your garden. Fine. Happy to do so. My *giardino* was in Italy.

Once we knew we wanted to move to Italy I had to finesse the notice period. On the day you give notice, it is the company's decision as to whether you work some or all of the notice period. Since I was making it clear that I was in effect, "retiring" and moving to Italy, I was not a threat to go off and join a competitor. So my guess was that they were not going to send me home on garden leave on the day I gave notice.

By the same token, I knew they would not ask

me to work the entire year of my notice period. I had been around the business world long enoug to know what happens whenever someone announces that he or she is leaving or changing jobs "in six-month's time". It doesn't work. You are a lame duck the minute it is announced you are leaving. People start jockeying for your parking space. They start measuring your office for new curtains. Your authority diminishes perceptively and immediately the minute change is announced. I used this to my benefit. I was happy to work part of my notice period but I wanted to be under the Tuscan sun by summer.

I flew to Barcelona, home of our parent company, in late January 2005, to give notice to my boss. He wasn't completely surprised, as my counterpart in the US had given notice a few month's earlier. And it wasn't every day when I called him up and said, "Can I fly down to see you tomorrow? We have to talk."

We were pretty much on the same page. The company was at a critical juncture trying to refinance some serious debt and while my boss accepted my resignation verbally, he asked me to put my notice letter back in my briefcase for a month or so until the refinancing was in place.

A short time later, we both agreed that we would announce my decision to leave at the end of March, and that I would work one more quarter so that I would be responsible for delivering our half-year results. All companies are driven by quarterly results and ours was no different. My last day of work would be June 30th. I would be on garden leave for the remaining six months of my notice period. My garden leave would be spent trying out new recipes in the *forno*.

Lucca here we come.

We found a wonderful family from Australia who agreed to rent our house on a long-term basis. On July 6th, 2005 we spent our last day in our home in London. Debbie and I were going through dozens of plastic tubs, deciding what to throw away and what to keep. My patience was wearing thin, as instead of rifling through a tub of papers and saying "keep it" or "chuck it", Debbie was propped up against a bedroom wall, going through old class folders page by page. "Oh, look at Billy's artwork back in 3rd grade. He was adorable. I have to save this." Just before midnight, I hoisted the final box into the attic and we climbed into an uncomfortable minicab for the ninety-minute trip to Gatwick airport, where we would get six hours sleep before catching our one-way flight to our new home.

We settled into la Casa Gialla and were thankful every day for being able to live in this little bit of paradise. Two years after we moved, I sat with pride looking at our financial situation. Even after giving up our jobs, our net worth had increased by 20%. I tempered my smugness with the knowledge that to do a net worth statement, you have to convert everything into a common currency. Being an American by birth, I always converted everything back to US dollars. Some of our 20% increase was due to exchange rate gains, but even so, our assets were increasing in value at a rate faster than our spending. I was a happy camper, making pizzas and not worrying about money.

While I was enjoying *la bella vita* during those first two years in Lucca, I was feeling that sense of loss that comes from when you leave a great job where you were the boss. I missed the everyday excitement of deals done and competitors vanquished. I missed the camaraderie of having a drink after work with my mates.

As I frequently joked to my friends, "I used to be the CEO of a £45 million per year business with 650 employees. Now I am in the No. 2 position in my own home."

I was ready for some action. Enter Anderò Srl.

Chapter 3 -- The Builder, the Banker, and the Geometra

The Builder

As we plotted our Anderò strategy in the spring of 2007, we knew we needed to put together a professional team to work along side us. Nicola Padrino and his extended family moved from Sicily to the Lucca area 25 years ago. When you ask him why, he goes slightly quiet and just says that he knew he was going to be in the construction business. And if he had stayed in Sicily, his business and his life would not have been his own.

The Mafia's participation in industries such as construction and waste management is well documented. What projects you worked on, how much you were paid, and how much you were expected to pay to others, was tightly controlled in the Sicilian construction industry. Nicola wanted a safer life for his family. In short, he moved to Tuscany to escape from the Sicilian Mafia.

He and his partner and their sons, daughters, and other family members came here to be independent and to build a successful construction company. When I watch Nicola and his wife proudly celebrate the wedding of their daughter, or the birth of a grandchild, or host a *Pasquetta* party (the day after Easter) for 50 of their friends, I know he has achieved his goal. Everything he builds is done to the highest standards with the best materials. He is a proud and noble man.

He came to us through Lou Codardo. When Lou successfully bought and sold a couple of houses during the boom times of the early 2000s, Nicola was his builder. He and his team are more than builders; they are artisans. On more than one occasion, I have watched them turn a pile of rocks into a spectacular stone wall with beautifully framed windows and doors, without a piece of paper or a plan in front of them. As the wall is being built they will look at the next space available, look at their pile of rubble, pick up a large stone, knock a little piece off a corner or two, and slip it beautifully into place. Their intermingling of different types and colors of stone is artistically intentional. Red bricks are used to create arched doorways and window frames that are miniature works of art all by themselves.

And the quality of the interiors – sometimes I had a problem with the quality; I thought the quality was too good. Nicola could not cut corners on a building project to save his life. As il Borghetto was going up, I was continually amazed at the multiple layers of materials that went into making a wall. They started out with double layers of cinder block with scraps of old tile thrown in as some form of ancient recycling method. Then stucco on all sides and not just a thin layer. The final internal walls measure a half-meter in some places. My big joke to Nicola on many an occasion was, "Could you please stop making the walls so thick? The apartments are getting smaller by the minute!" His response was a shrug and a smile and a,"*Così è come lo facciamo.*" This is how we do it.

Nicola was more than our builder. He was just as excited as we were about our *Building Dreams in Tuscany* concept and he pressed us from the beginning to be a minority partner with Anderò. We brought him in as a 20% partner for all Anderò projects. As part of his investment, Nicola agreed to bill us for only 80% of his costs during the construction phase, taking his remaining 20% only when we sold something. He even brought some investment money into the company from his friends back in Sicily. It was his vote of confidence in us and in our plan that helped my vision for the company grow with each passing day. We were going to be big players in the Tuscan holiday home market and Nicola was just the partner we needed to be successful.

The Banker

When Debbie and I bought our house in 2003 the banks in Italy were fighting over themselves to lend money to foreign investors. So many Brits were buying homes in Tuscany that part of it was nicknamed *Chiantishire*. British banks like Barclays opened offices in Italy to get in on the action. We easily got a mortgage for our house even though it was intended to be a second home as we were not planning to live in Italy full time when we applied for the loan. It was a holiday home, but no one seemed concerned that if we stopped making the payments, it would be pretty hard to chase us back in the UK. Banks were flush with money. Their attitude was, "Let's give this guy his loan and go out and do another one."

It was the same on the commercial lending side of the bank. Several banks were throwing big commissions to the mortgage broker we were working with to bring them customers – any customers – so they could approve another mortgage. The banks were excited to work with us as we held the promise of bringing them six buyers for il Borghetto's apartments and five buyers for the homes at la Porcellaia in Arsina, all foreigners who would need a mortgage. Our mortgage broker also helped me refinance our home twice in the first three years we lived here, as the deals kept getting better.

So it was with great congeniality that Lou and I were greeted at our first meeting with the bank recommended by our mortgage broker, in their beautiful headquarters on Piazza San Michele in the heart of Lucca. We laid out our business plan, told them about our two current projects, and shared with them our ideas for acquiring more properties to renovate. They couldn't have been more co-operative and in hindsight, our loan approval was the fastest decision that I've ever seen a bank make in Italy.

We were pleased that they were going to lend

us construction money of €600,000 ($800,000) for il Borghetto and €1,300,000 ($1,750,000) for la Porcellaia. We were a bit puzzled that the il Borghetto loan represented only 50% of the construction costs and the Arsina loan was for 80% of the costs, but they said not to worry. "It's all a loan to Anderò, so if you need to move money from one project to the other, it is not a problem."

This easy money only increased our appetite to take on more projects and more risk. We were hungry to find more abandoned barns and derelict villas which could be converted into beautiful holiday homes. Most of these properties were not listed with any agent. It was all word of mouth, from farmer to farmer. We looked at everything from small barns to ruins that were so large that we had thoughts of opening a luxury hotel. It was late 2007 and the world economy was booming. Our mantra of "Build it and they will come" seemed like the no-brainer strategy of the year. All we needed was to find a great *geometra* and we would be off and running.

The *Geometra*

How do I describe the *geometra's* role in Italy? They are a cross between a designer and an architect, but their true purpose in life is to be the navigators of the bureaucracy. They create the thousands of documents needed to present to the *Comune* and the *Belle Arte* to get permission to build anything. I have never seen so many mountains of paper in all my life. You need planning permission in Italy for almost everything. Want to put a garden shed on your property? Does it have a permanent, cement base? Then you need planning permission. Want to build a pizza oven in your back yard? Add a window? Then just send your paperwork to the *Comune*, in triplicate, and wait. Patiently. It took us 28 months from the time we bought the ruin at il Borghetto to the day when we received our *permesso*, the building permit. I was told that no one even looks at an application for a big project for the first few months after you submit it to the *Comune*. You join the queue. I guess they figure your application is like a fine bottle of wine -- it will get better with age.

Lou had worked with Attilio Serpente as his *geometra* for many years. Smiling, likeable, with just enough English to be able to explain the unfathomable process to us, we were all happy to press forward with him leading the charge for our building permits for il Borghetto and la Porcellaia. We were impressed with the dozens of detailed documents that we occasionally had to sit down and sign before they went off to the *Comune*. Attilio seemed well-organized and well-connected.

While his floor plans were a series of uninspiring boxes, he made them look pretty with a few software design tools. He was even better at coming up with a financial model that showed us making 40% profit on each project that we discussed with him. In hindsight, all he did was to add up all the costs associated with acquiring and building a project and add a 40% margin to come up with the selling prices. Although they looked a bit high, this was 2007 when people were still flocking to Tuscany and prices were still going up. If we had any second thoughts they were quickly replaced with, "Even if we have a little price erosion, we will still make 30% and we're laughing." In my euphoric state, it never occurred to me to do a hard analysis of what would happen if the erosion turned into an avalanche. Attilio drew up the designs for il Borghetto and la Porcellaia and he sent the mountains of paperwork off to the *Comune*. We were off and running. *Avanti!*

A couple of my friends questioned how much we were being charged by Attilio, but since it was a fixed price, taking us from design to occupancy permit, we were happy to know in advance there would be no cost overruns. We were going to sell the apartments for a 40% profit even with his bill included. What could go wrong?

The confidence I had in our property development business spilled over into my private life. I felt proud as I thought about the 20% increase I was seeing in our net worth two years after leaving London. I was feeling flush, which made me the perfect customer when my

neighbors came to call one autumn day in
2007.

Chapter 4 -- An Offer We Can't Refuse

La Casa Gialla is small, built on the side of a hill, and the plot of land surrounding it isn't much bigger. We have a swimming pool that starts about twenty feet from our kitchen window, because Giulio, who built our house, didn't buy enough land for the garden. Only six feet from two sides of the pool there were two, ten-foot high stone walls, holding back the earth as the hill spilled steeply down in front of our house. Those walls were our property line. We barely had room for two chairs around the pool. About five feet above the pool, there was a small terrace and our *forno*. The only outdoor entertaining space we had was a table for eight in front of the *forno*. We were so mesmerized by the view when we bought the house, we didn't realize what little land we owned.

Not to worry. Our Italian neighbors knew an opportunity when they saw it.

Two years after we arrived, our neighbors came to call. As you do whenever this happens in Italy, you offer them a *Prosecco* or a coffee and you sit around together and have a chat. *"Avete bisogno di alcuni alberi di ulivo,"* they told us. You need some olive trees. Absolutely right. We were probably the only people with a home in the hills who had to buy their olive oil from the supermarket. Disgraceful. Any proper Italian home in the hills should have dozens of olive trees, if not a small vineyard. Our neighbors were here to solve our problem.

Land with olive trees on it isn't normally that expensive, unless you are a foreigner and the land in question is attached to your property.

Then the price goes up. They offered to sell us a piece of land about 40 meters by 30 meters in size, just under one-third of an acre. It had thirty olive trees on it, plus four beautiful pear trees and a couple of fig trees. It was in beautiful condition as they had been harvesting the olives and other fruit trees for decades. We said we would think about it (mustn't appear too eager) and then our little gathering ended with smiles, handshakes and kisses. No mention of the price.

Italians really don't like talking about money. They are reluctant to tell you the price of anything too early in the conversation. They consider it *brutta figura* (boorish manners – the literal translation of "ugly figure" says it better) to focus on the price of anything. If you ask for a *sconto,* a discount, in most shops they are quick to offer one. Many times they will give you a *sconto* without you having to ask, or they round €62.50 down to €60, as a kind gesture. They really want you to be happy after you pay. Everyone should walk away satisfied. I love that aspect of Italian culture.

I needed some lawyerly advice. During our first months in Lucca we were connected at the hip to our friends Doris and Doug. We needed their help for everything; from setting up our utilities contracts, to choosing a cell phone provider. We needed a cable TV contract, a good butcher, the best bakery, and reliable doctors and dentists. Our Italian was so limited that we had difficulty carrying on a business conversation with anyone.

Doris's cousin, Franco, was an easy choice for our lawyer. And Franco's wife, Cristina, became our banker. Networking is everything in Italy and we had found a great one. Doris and Doug have acted in this capacity for a dozen or more newcomers like us who came to live here without knowing how things work or how to get things done. Their generosity knows no bounds.

I told Franco about the offer to buy some land around our house and we had a follow-up meeting with the neighbors, at which point the price finally came out. €25,000 ($34,000). Yikes! For thirty olive trees? Wouldn't it be easier to keep buying olive oil at the store? Surely this was a price for *stranieri* (foreigners). Surely I could ask for a *sconto*.

Surprisingly, Franco sided with the neighbors. "Yes, the price is high but it will add at least that much value, or more, to your house to have this olive grove that is attached to your property," was his explanation. He also told me it was their pension fund that they were trying to top up. What was I to do? I didn't want to come across as the ugly American, trying to beat up these poor pensioners to get a lower price. So I trusted Franco's judgment, sighed, and agreed to their number. That whooshing sound you hear is the money leaving my bank account.

We needed to record the sale legally with the *notaio*. Now if I could pick a job to have in Italy, it would be a *notaio*, the person who acts as the recorder of deeds. It's like having a license to print money. Whether you are buying or selling; whether the property is a €10 million villa or a €25,000 land purchase, you must do it with the *notaio*. How to pick one?

Well, it doesn't matter very much to them. It is a private sector job, but the government sets them up with protected territories. One *notaio* for every so many thousands of residents. So the supply never outstrips the demand. I've used the same *notaio* for a dozen years now and I'm not sure which facet of his job I admire more: his palatial office with thirty-foot high ceilings and beautiful frescoes; or, his always beautifully tailored Armani suits. His impossibly heavy and expensive pens are there to make you feel important as you sign everything in triplicate at the closing. You have to give the pen back before you leave.

At the closing for the piece of land we were buying, I was amazed that five people showed up to sign on behalf of the sellers. It had taken quite a bit of time to sort out the boundaries of the property, defined only by small ditches built into all the hillsides to help with the drainage of rain water. It turned out this piece of land was part of a larger plot owned by many brothers, sisters, and cousins of the Bevilacqua family. I knew our hillside was populated with many Bevilacquas. It's pretty obvious when the street we live on is Via dei Bevilacqua. I wonder how that happened.

So one by one, the five Bevilacqua family members signed, I signed, and then I wrote some more checks out to Franco and the *notaio*. They charge a percentage of the value of the transaction so I got off relatively light with this purchase. Their fee for a €10 million villa must be obscene. The work required for the €10 million villa sale compared to my little olive tree purchase isn't that much more. Like I said, I'd love to be a *notaio*.

We used our new land to great advantage. We found an engineer to draw up a clever plan to give us more flat space for entertaining around the pool. We used the hillside to build a 6 x 6 meter *magazzino* (storage room) into the hill, such that the flat roof would be at the same level as the pool. We covered up the original stone walls and built what they call a *terra armata*, an earthen wall, cleverly built with steel mesh and dirt to provide stability at a much lower cost than if we had built more stone walls.

Then we built a *pergola* on top of the *magazzino* and landscaped the hillside above it with 250 aubelia plants, which bloom throughout the late summer and autumn with pretty white flowers. We chose two wisteria plants to attach to the pergola and in two years they had totally covered the top to give us shade from the hot summer sun. Lunches and dinners next to the pool, under the pergola, with pizzas and other treats coming from the *forno*, became regular events during the summer months.

We love our little la Casa Gialla and the outdoor spaces have created memorable moments over our 13 years here. Birthday parties for 35 people, pizza fests, olive harvests -- we treasure these memories made with friends and family. With this new addition to our home-life secured, it was time to turn my attention to Anderò. Let's get on with *Building Dreams in Tuscany. Avanti!*

Chapter 5 -- The Dark Years

In hindsight, if ever there was a phrase guaranteed to strike fear in the heart of any businessman, be it in the US, Britain, or Italy, it would be, "I started my property development business in 2007."

Just one year after we set up Anderò, dark clouds started to gather on the horizon. We had plunked down €1.2 million on two projects that looked like surefire winners in 2007. Il Borghetto and la Porcellaia combined were going to give us eleven homes to sell to eleven families looking to capture their vision of the Tuscan dream. Our business model of buying the land for €1,000 per square meter; building everything, including the pool and landscaping for €2,000 per square meter; and selling the apartments for €4,500 per square meter seemed simple and profitable – until it wasn't.

Dark Cloud No. 1 – The Financial Meltdown

I am going to have a difficult time writing this part of the story without dropping a serious number of f-bombs. Because I am angry. You would think that as a former business executive, I could be ruthless; ready and willing to throw anyone under the bus to achieve my goals, earn a big bonus and top up my stock options. Don't get me wrong, I strongly believe in the saying that "Capitalism is the worst economic system in the world -- except for all the other economic systems." Capitalism can bring out the best in innovation and personal achievement. America and other countries have shown leadership to the world by bringing exciting and life-changing new products and services to the market.

It can also incentivize senior executives in every business sector, especially banking, to screw over the rest of the world in exchange for obscene personal profits.

Which is exactly what the American banking industry did in the mid 2000s. Just watch *The Big Short*, or *Margin Call*, or *Too Big to Fail*, and these movies can explain the great financial mortgage scam hidden behind the non-descript instruments called CDOs and MBSs better than I can. Their blatant greed and sophisticated shell game ruined the lives of millions of people. It indirectly helped to ruin mine, as the housing and economic crisis that came crashing down in 2008 was not confined to the US.

People who had a net worth of $10 million one day and €2 million the next suddenly decided they could do without that second home they were planning to buy in Tuscany. The investment banker who was worth €100 million one day, but now only worth €20 million decided that she didn't need a third retreat to go along with her homes in New

York and Paris. The ripple effect hit every country in Western Europe. Property values in Central London were probably the only ones that held their value, which was still a setback from increasing by between 5% and 10% per year, as they had done for long spurts of time over the past thirty years. In spite of the ten-year financial downturn that was to come, our owning a house in London from 2001 to 2013 was the best investment I had ever made.

The direct hit that we took in Italy was easy to measure. Tuscany had always been the romantic jewel in the world of real estate and it prided itself in having the highest prices per square meter for countryside homes in all of Italy. My over-confident wisdom of the time was that I thought of Tuscany like I do London. If a recession hits, prices might stop climbing for a short time, but climb eventually they will. I spent from 2008 – 2010 with these rose-colored-glass thoughts firmly planted in my head.

So it was shocking to see prices fall dramatically here in Tuscany after a few years of the worldwide economic recession. I know there might not be much sympathy out there for us just because our target market of multi-millionaires had dried up. But I'm also channeling a lot of anger speaking up for people I know in the US whose mortgages were suddenly far higher than the value of their home. The same banks who were lending money at 100% and more of the value of a home, which exacerbated the economic crisis when the fraud was exposed and the homes were devalued, then turned into bastards when people came to them begging for re-financing help. And none of the major players on Wall Street who perpetrated this fraud went to jail.

There, I got through that without a single f-bomb.

No, I can't do it. Sorry. Fuck those greedy bastards. May they burn in hell.

Dark Cloud No. 2 - Kevin the Rainmaker

We started the company with a grand vision of becoming a big player in the holiday home market. Lou had success building and selling a couple of his homes and our plan was to scale-up his successes by having multiple projects on the go at any one time. We had spent a lot of time inspecting old barns and talking to farmers whose outbuildings weren't quite on the market, but who would sell for the right price.

Ten years earlier farmers were selling their barns to outsiders for €50,000 ($67,500), a bargain price. Once they discovered that people were building modest but beautiful homes on the site of their old barn, and making a fortune in the process, prices rose quickly until you had to add a zero to your offer. Still, if you looked hard enough you could find some available properties in beautiful locations, so we made a few offers and had several other projects in our sights in the first year of Anderò. Now all we needed was money.

In those first two years we thought we had a financier in Lou's friend, Kevin the Rainmaker. A technology entrepreneur, Kevin was our designated money man. Lou made several mumbled promises to Kevin that he could join us as a full partner and he became an enthusiastic supporter of Anderò from the start. When Raul came to us after our first year and said that he wanted out, Lou convinced Kevin to plunk down €100,000 to buy Raul's shares in the company. The fact that we never legally recorded this ownership change was something that Lou tip-toed around, with little resistance from Kevin. Lou convinced me that Kevin was fine with this arrangement and as he had the personal relationship with Kevin, I let it be. After all, we were all going to get rich developing real estate in Tuscany. Build it and they will come!

Years later, it didn't matter that Kevin wasn't legally made a co-captain of the Titanic. All our original seed money went up in smoke. Il Cubano was the only smart one who got out before the economy moved into full-crash territory in 2008 and 2009. Kevin was unable to raise the money we expected from him, save for one of his friends who later turned his unsecured investment in Anderò into a down payment on an apartment. It was a blessing in disguise that Kevin could not raise more money because we would have used that money to buy up several more barns and restoration projects, and we would have ended up losing millions of other people's money.

Dark Cloud No. 3 - The Bank

My annoyances with the bank over their lack of customer service in the lobby when dealing with my personal account became insignificant as the years went by, when the global housing meltdown, precipitated by the greed in the US banking industry, took hold in the rest of the world. Bank losses in Italy from "non-performing loans", the cute euphemism for when customers stop making their payments, were piling up. For several years, with great difficulty, we kept making our interest payments on time every six months. Even so, the congeniality we once saw from our bankers turned to suspicion as we had not pre-sold any apartments at il Borghetto or la Porcellaia.

By 2009 the financial crisis had really taken hold and my local bank contacts became morose. You could sense the gloom in the executive offices on the upper floors of our bank in Piazza San Michelle in the historic center of Lucca. We were put on their "watch list" when we wisely decided not to start construction on la Porcellaia, even after we got our building permit. We tore down the pig farm and stopped. We didn't have the money to build our approved project there, but more importantly, the financial crisis and lack of buyers made it obvious that we didn't need another five apartments to sell on top of the six we were trying to find owners for at il Borghetto.

We would have been woefully underfunded had we gone ahead and would have had both projects on hold and half-built if we had started la Porcellaia. It was better to complete our first project at the expense of the second one. But we had taken the first tranche of money for la Porcellaia and the bank was concerned about how we were going to repay the loan if we didn't follow through and build it.

One annoying aspect of the Italian banking crisis was that every time a decision had to be made from 2010 onward, no one could make that decision in Lucca. If we had the simplest of questions, such as requesting the next tranche of money as called for in our loan agreement, our contacts at the bank, even if they had a fancy title, could not make the decision. First it was sent off to Livorno or Florence, their regional offices. You knew it was really serious when Florence sent it to Rome for a decision. God help you if it went to Rome. It was weeks and sometimes months before we heard back from them. I was starting to believe that our local bank VP had to write to Rome to ask permission to go to the bathroom.

I don't know how to explain this problem of slow decision-making and missed deadlines in Italian life. Many people think that countries like Spain and Italy, who shut down for lunch for two or three hours every day, must be napping or are lazy. This is not true. It is a cultural tradition that you go home and have lunch with your family. Offices and shops open again around 3:30 p.m. and the workday continues until 7:00 or 8:00 p.m. Small family businesses don't have the extra staff necessary to keep their businesses open for twelve hours a day. It's an accepted rhythm of life here and everyone puts in a full day's work, just not in the way that the UK or America does it. We know many hard-working Italians running small businesses who give their all to make them successful. They just do it in the context of our local rhythm of life.

No, the problem is more a lack of urgency in most things related to government, construction, and banking. Part of it is cultural. The pace of life here is relaxed, healthy and full of interpersonal relationships. I have lost count of the times when something could have been explained to me over the phone in five minutes, but instead, "Come see me," says my *geometra* or my *commercialista* (accountant) or my *imprenditore* (builder). "Come see me, I want to explain it to you." They do, and then we go have a coffee. This is one of the Italians' most endearing traits. They genuinely care about people. They want to do business face to face. For the most part they are trying to do the right thing. But without a sense of urgency. And if this lack urgency means I don't get through the five things on my "To Do" list for any given day, well, my expectations were just set too high, weren't they?

In the first few years I lived here, I would go out on my motorbike in the morning with that list of five things to do. Simple things: the dry cleaner; pick up something at the hardware store; grocery store; the bank; and stop to pick up some fertilizer for the olive trees.

The first setback was the thirty-minute queue at the post office. The Italian post office provides more services than I can count, including many banking services. So you might be third in the queue with two windows open and think you're in good shape. But some of these services take twenty minutes to conduct. I spend my thirty minutes waiting in frustration; organizing in my mind how it should work, with dedicated windows for people who just want to buy a stamp. They have tried doing that but the system breaks down when you are in a Post Office with six windows and only two of them are staffed.

I finally get to the window, pay my two utility bills in two minutes and with just a small amount of steam coming out of my ears, I'm off to the second task on my list, the hardware store. "Ah, we don't have the part you are looking for, but wait here because I might have something in the back that you can use." We chat, we check out a few possible solutions, and we decide to order the correct part and I'll come back another day. Another twenty minutes gone. This goes on until one o'clock is approaching and I only have three of my five items accomplished. I am racing to the fourth place, dangerously zipping around cars on my scooter, trying to get there before they close for lunch.

I sigh and give up. I pop into my favorite *panificio* (bakery) just behind the San Michele church, buy some fresh focaccia for lunch, and leave two items on my To Do list for tomorrow.

There is only one deadline that is so powerful, so frightening in the consequences of missing it, that the Italians will move heaven and earth to meet it. The only deadline that rises to this level of importance? Mamma. You never want to disappoint mamma. This really hit home with me during Doug and Doris's massive renovation project of the derelict stone millhouse, il Mulino, they purchased just before their wedding.

The renovations were complex and endless, with Doug doing most of the heavy lifting, but needing help with electricity and plumbing. Custom-made windows had to be installed before the heat could go in, to make the house habitable for family and friends. Well in advance of when they thought everything would be ready, dates were set for the visit of Doug's mom from the States and the unveiling of the renovated mill house.

One week prior to her arrival, panic was setting in. There was no running water. The plumber was procrastinating. And then, not as part of any strategy or manipulation, but in desperation just the same, Doris said to the workman, "But it has to be ready by next week... *la mamma di Douglas arriva!* " Doug's mom is coming! Doris might as well have said the Pope was on his way. More workers showed up, the pace picked up, and 24 hours before *la mamma* arrived from Minnesota, hot water was running and the windows were in place.

For the past ten years, whenever any of us have been frustrated with having to wait for something to be fixed, we try to summon up our courage to use the *"la mamma di Douglas arriva"* technique to push through the barriers. I don't know of anyone who has actually done it, but God, it is tempting. It's a shame that it would never work at my bank.

As the housing crisis and financial scandal took a deeper hold in 2009 and 2010, we faced our first crisis. We were running out of money just one year into the building of il Borghetto. The bank construction loan only paid us in tranches of 20% at a time as we built the project and they withheld the final 20% until construction was finished. The loan was only for about 50% of the total construction costs so we needed additional help.

In the first of what would grow to be a long list of disappointments with our bank, it reneged on its promise that we would be able to move some of the approved la Porcellaia loan to the il Borghetto project. Our contacts at the bank went blank when we reminded them of their promises. We dreaded each meeting with them as we tried to hold them to their original commitment and they kept asking, "When are you going to sell some of the apartments?"

But at least we had other good members on our team. We had our *geometra*, who was going to fast-track our building permits so we could move on with *Building Dreams in Tuscany* for foreign buyers. Lou Codardo had a good track record with him for years. We were in good hands, right?

Dark Cloud No. 4 - The Geometra

OK, maybe not such good hands. Attilio had been making a nice living working with *stranieri*. His charm and the English language skills, remember? When the property market inevitably screeched to a near halt, even in Tuscany, Attilio's work dried up. Then he started acting strangely. He asked for his scheduled payments a bit too far in advance. He asked to borrow a few thousand euros from time to time. He finally approached us and reduced his bill as we neared the end of the first project, if we would pay him the discounted amount immediately. He was obviously using our money to cover other expenses and we were too far down the road with him to dump him and move on. Besides, we had paid him for the entire job. We might as well see it through to the occupancy permit.

And then his big sin. He stole money from us.

Cash. It wouldn't be possible to steal a large sum of cash in most countries. But Italy's economy runs on cash and there are several reasons why this has developed over the years. It starts with Italy being one of the poorer economic performers in Europe in recent years, even though we have the 9th biggest economy in the world. One strain on the economy is that Italians live longer than those in other EU countries, and the percent of Italy's GNP that goes to pay pensioners is 10%, the highest in Europe. That is because in Italy, you used to be able to retire after 35 years of work with about 90% of your final salary as a pension - for the rest of your life. If you started working at age 20, you could fully retire at age 55. Combine that with the glories of the Mediterranean diet; the vast amounts of extra virgin olive oil consumed, the moderate amounts of red wine they drink (only with meals), and these people are living into their 90s without ever missing a Sunday *passeggiata*. The full salary pension they collect along the way sucks a lot of the life out of the Italian treasury.

Another contributing factor is that Italy has one of the lowest birthrates in Europe, which further stymies the economy by having fewer numbers of workers entering the workforce to pay taxes.

Ah, taxes. Now we arrive at the real crisis. There is a massive problem with Italy's tax collection system. Avoiding having to pay taxes is pretty much a national sport here. They do it by using cash as much as possible. Italy has run for decades on the black economy, known as *nero*. Everyone participates in the *nero* economy and in a vicious cycle as the government struggles to collect enough money in taxes to run the country, it raises taxes, which encourages more black market activity. *IVA*, Italy's value added tax rate, is currently 22%, charged on just about everything we buy except for food.

"Do you want a *fattura* (invoice) or do you want to pay with cash?" is a question that comes up regularly from Italian businesses and individuals. No one wants to pay IVA. The government is wise to this, of course, so there is this lovely orchestrated dance around the system. If you are a housepainter, you buy paint and supplies from a building supplier and you pay tax on what you buy. The government expects you to use those materials to paint someone's house, give them an official invoice, and charge IVA to the customer. The game that is played is, "How much do I have to report as taxable income to keep the government off my back?"

The result is this: the housepainter agrees to paint your house for €5,000. He gives you an invoice for €2,500 plus 22% VAT and you pay him the remaining €2,500 in *nero* – cash - under the table. He reports income of €2,500 to paint your house and pays income taxes on that. You save the 22% IVA on half of the job so you and the painter both win.

The government is trying to crack down on this and they are making some progress, but it is a game that is played every day all over the country. When the plumbers, electricians, carpenters, and gardeners come to our house to do some work, the response to my "I don't need a receipt, may I pay you in cash?" is always greeted with a *"Certo!"* ("Certainly!"). They give me a little discount and everyone is happy. Except for the taxman.

The fact that the economy runs on large sums of cash means that most businesses and many homeowners have a safe built into the wall of their offices and homes to hide the cash. If your house is ever burgled in Italy, they don't take passports or even computers. They look behind every picture hanging on the wall for your safe. They only want gold jewelry and cash.

I don't remember where it came from, but it came to pass that some of Anderò's cash happened to be stored in the wall safe in Atillio Serpente's office.

We were meeting with Attilio one day in his office and at the end of the meeting, we asked to take some of the cash with us for our builder. All of a sudden, he jumped up and exclaimed, "I'm late for a meeting." We all rushed out and Lou and I looked at each other quizzically. At the next meeting we forced Attilio to admit that he had taken our money to pay some of his bills, but there was fresh money coming in any day now to replenish it.

When Attilio couldn't give us a date for when the money would be returned, we demanded that he sign a confession, stating that he had taken the money and that it would be repaid. This turned out to be an insurance policy for us because we all knew that if we took this letter to the police or, worse for him I suspect, the governing body of *geometras*, his license would be revoked. We got our money back. Then we fired Attilio. He left town and I heard he went to Brazil to try to start over there. It turned out we were not his only victims.

The second disaster is that Attilio never did the work at the end of the project to get our occupancy permit. There was another mountain of paperwork required to submit to the *Comune* when construction was completed, to prove that what you built was not one meter bigger than what you had permission to build. It was at this final step in the process where

Attilio just disappeared. Slippery doesn't begin to describe him. "The paperwork has been at the *Comune* for three weeks now. It should be signed off by the end of the month." He didn't say which month. He didn't say which year. But I guess the fact that he hadn't submitted the final paperwork in the first place made those two questions moot. It cost us tens of thousands of euros to hire a new *geometra* to finish the approval process for which we had already paid Attilio.

Well before Attilio betrayed us he also talked us into letting a friend of his, who turned out to be his mistress, do a promotional CD for our marketing efforts. Her renderings of the interiors were amateurish and the sound track in the background was overly-dramatic. It was more appropriate for showing off the Vatican than trying to sell six apartments. Then she presented us with a bill for €10,000 and was incensed when we wouldn't pay it. She went to a personal friend of hers, who happened to be the equivalent of the town sheriff, and he called us into his office late one night on "unofficial business... I am just trying to help a friend resolve her dispute with you." Yeah, right. He stopped just short of slapping his gun down on his oversized desk. Lou and I had trusted Attilio that this woman was reputable and competent. In my mind she was neither. Because it was the early days of Anderò and we had some marketing money set aside, I just wanted this ugly episode to be behind us. After a lot of shouting and arm-waving, we agreed to pay her a lesser amount.

The journey from buying the derelict centuries-old ruin that we transformed into il Borghetto in San Gennaro was a long and tedious one. I'm not afraid of lions and tigers and bears. Crooked *geometras*, lying bankers, and stifling bureaucracy, combined with an attitude of "*piano, piano*" (slowly, slowly), now those are the things that strike fear in my heart.

It was about this time when the phrase, "under the Tuscan thumb" first popped into my mind. Our *geometra* was stealing from us. The economy, led by the collapse of the housing market, was tanking. The banks, who had started out so friendly, were starting to badger us and withhold previously promised money. The pressure of all that was getting to me. On top of all that, my partner, Lou, had a few character flaws that were adding to my stress levels.

Il Codardo

A few character flaws? What can I say about a business partner who has a moral compass without a needle?

No, that's not the right image. It's more like a compass with one of those needles that spins around in circles at a rate of speed so fast that....

No, that's not right either. Ah, yes. Here it is: Lou has a moral compass with multiple needles pointing in every direction. Because when it came to making the decision to either stay with his wife or live with the Mistress, he ticked the box: ☒ All of the above

Lou had been spending most of his time in Lucca for the past ten years, while he also had a home in Toronto. His wife was with him here, until she grew tired of the hot summers. She returned to Toronto and eventually they built a new home there, which created the perfect opportunity for him to spend most of his time in Italy without her. He found a local Brazilian girl friend and all was well in his life.

But then the Mistress reappeared; a Canadian woman who was his mistress decades earlier and now they had found each other again. They had a secret rendezvous in London and rekindled their hot affair. She came to Italy to be with him on more than one occasion, risking her marriage and her relationship with her ten-year old daughter.

She eventually demanded to know where the relationship was going. She couldn't keep living a lie with her husband. Lou had no such moral qualms. He thought the arrangement was perfect. She called him a coward frequently.

Finally, he agreed that he was in love with her and wanted only to be with her. He said he would divorce his wife, face the wrath of his two grown daughters in their 30s, who hadn't quite grown up yet, and live with the Mistress in Tuscany forever, in a new house they would build together.

Having pledged their undying love for each other, they made a pact to fly back to their respective Canadian cities, to simultaneously announce that they wanted a divorce, so they could walk bravely into the future together. It was a nice plan, but the execution was a little faulty. Lou didn't quite live up to his end of the deal.

The day after the planned announcements, there was a telephone call. I'm sure it went something like this: "So, I told my husband," said the Mistress. "He's angry, hurt, but knows this is the end for us. How did it go for you?"

"Uh….well…it wasn't a good time to tell her. The girls are in a sensitive place right now and I know they will be angry and I don't want to lose them." He hadn't said a word to his wife. The Mistress was furious.

In the months after that dark night, Lou somehow convinced the Mistress that they should go ahead with their life together in Italy, including going 50/50 on building a luxury villa in the hills south of Lucca. He would deal with the wife later. Lou must have some mystical powers with women, because the Mistress bought his lies and they struggled along in Italy for another year or so before it all came crashing down.

With all our other business problems swirling around me, Lou's instability was starting to wear thin. His ability to lie to his family and others didn't bode well for our partnership. Was he capable of turning on me, too? Surely there must be someone I can trust here.

Ah yes, our Sicilian builder.

Chapter 6 -- The Rock

Through these first few turbulent years, Nicola Padrino was a rock. Stopping and starting construction twice on il Borghetto because we kept running out of money caused countless problems for him in planning the construction phases. Even those disruptions were not what kept him awake at night. There was a second and much more significant element to Nicola's participation in Anderò. Shortly after we formed the company, he went to his friends in Sicily and raised additional money to invest in Anderò. This investment was totally unsecured. It was officially documented through what we call an *Associazione in Partecipazione*. This is a legally registered contract that allows investors who are not owners to participate in the financing of a company. The contract lays out the terms for paying back investors their principal investment plus a share of the profit. We were offering generous percentages to potential investors as money became more difficult to raise; basically giving the first profits to our investors, with Lou, Kevin and I taking our share last.

Several people invested in us using this instrument and they all knew the risks. Their loans were unsecured. The return of their investment plus profit was totally dependent on the profitability of Anderò Srl, a limited liability company. When we booked a loss in excess of $1 million in 2013, Anderò's chances of ever making a profit were gone. None of our unsecured investors had any hope of seeing the return of their investment. Including Nicola's friends in Sicily.

As the years have rolled by without Nicola

being able to repay a single euro of his friends' investment, I have seen the worry on his face at our regular lunch meetings. One day when I asked him what was going on, he told me that he was going to Sicily the next week to visit his family. He probably returns to his birthplace four or five times a year. This time, he knew he was going to have to meet with his investor friends, and explain once again why he couldn't repay the money. He was genuinely worried. On more than one occasion since then, after returning from Sicily, I ask him over lunch how it went. He holds an imaginary gun to his head and pulls the trigger. He wasn't talking suicide, and he was only half kidding.

The fact that we were never able to pay his final 20% of the construction costs meant that he has taken a big hit. He basically did years of work and the only benefit he got out of it was keeping his team of Sicilian builders employed. He and I are so close that he rarely brings it up anymore. He knows that if I could pay him I would. He appreciates the sacrifices I have made trying to get his final 20% for him.

In the summer of 2012, when we ran out of money for the second time during the construction of il Borghetto, I tried to put myself in his shoes. Here we have a builder who has bought into our company as a 20% partner; who has agreed to take less than what he is entitled to during the construction phase; who has brought in other investors and put his reputation and possibly more on the line; and now we have arrived at a point where we have run out of money and shut down construction, with only the foundation and the walls in place.

What would any other builder do? Sue me? What would a Sicilian builder do? Whack me? What did Nicola do? He invited Debbie and me to his daughter's wedding.

A Sicilian wedding is something to behold. We were honored to be the only non-Italians at a wedding of more than 100 people. No movie could have done it justice.

The ceremony was at 4:00 p.m. in a church in the village near Lucca where Nicola, his wife, and their extended families live. All their relatives and friends from Sicily came up for the wedding. Nicola is from a small town near Corleone. Yes, that Corleone. The small town from where Don Vito took his name when he moved to America in *The Godfather*. The bride and groom arrived in a horse-drawn carriage and we experienced the full-on Italian Catholic mass wedding ceremony.

After it was over we were invited back to their home for a few hours to relax, sip *Prosecco*, and get ready for the wedding reception. Did I say wedding reception? More like a marathon endurance contest. It was at a beautiful villa high in the hills overlooking the Lucca plain. On a beautiful, warm summer's night, we drank *Prosecco* outdoors by the pool and were served lovely antipasti and *Parmesan* cheese, which we dipped in the finest balsamic vinegar from Modena.

Italians never drink without eating. In all the years I have lived here I can count on the fingers of one hand the time I have seen an Italian drunk, and they were teenagers.

Italians never go into a bar and just drink.
They might go in and have one *Prosecco* on
their way home to dinner and no matter how
small the coffee bar is, there will always be
something on the bar to eat. From nuts and
chips to little pizza slices, mini-panini of
prosciutto crudo, and sometimes a bit of pasta or
rice, Italians just feel it is wrong to drink
without having something to eat. They don't
drink outside of meal times. They drink in
moderation. It's part of the reason why they
live so long, I'm sure.

Finally around 9:00 p.m., we were called to
dinner. If I knew what was in store for me I
would have brought a seat belt for my chair.

Overflowing platters of prosciutto and Sicilian
salami arrived first with bread and olive oil.
Then it was time to get serious. A lovely plate
of pasta with seafood arrived. Almost all
dinners in Italy, whether at home or in a
restaurant consist of a *primo* (first course), a
secondo (I don't need to translate this, do I?)
and then dessert. Sometimes you might have
antipasti before the *primo*. The *primo* is usually

pasta. The *secondo* is most always meat or fish.

So I was looking forward to the main course when another plate of pasta arrived, this one meat-based. Each region of Italy has a signature dish for which they are famous. In Emiglia Romagna it is spaghetti Bolognese. In our area it is *tordelli*, ravioli filled with a ragu of beef and pork, seasoned with a bit of nutmeg or cinnamon, and topped with a tomato/meat ragu. It is made by every *nonna* in the Lucca province and has been for hundreds of years. It is *squisito*. We tucked into this one with enthusiasm.

As the courses continued the bride and groom and some of the guests would jump up occasionally and have a dance. A great idea because looking back on it, it would have been hard to sit in one spot for four continuous hours doing nothing but eating.

Time for the *secondo*. Make that *secondi*. Plural. A lovely fish course arrived, *branzino* (sea bass) with roasted potatoes and veg. Now I'm starting to get full. We have moved on from our white wine and into some lovely reds as the courses have progressed. While Italian white wines have come along nicely over the years (a great *Vermentino* is clean, crisp and delicious), we are more famous for our reds, from the unpretentious table wines made from the *Sangiovese* grape that is prominent everywhere in Tuscany, to the more noble and sophisticated *Brunellos* and *Barolos*.

There is a brief interlude and we all get up for a dance. Then the lights are turned down and out of the kitchen come a team of waiters with overflowing platters of lobsters. Huge lobsters. They have been cracked open and the waiters fly around the room, placing a healthy chunk on everyone's plate. This is the *intermezzo* between the two *secondi*.

After we clean ourselves up from tackling the lobster, the second main course arrives. *Bistecca Fiorentina*. (Florentine beefsteak) Famous around the world, this beef from our local *Chianina* cattle is delicious. Always cut extra thick, charred on the outside, rare on the inside, it is served with rocket and *Parmesan*, with olive oil drizzled over the top. My eyes are starting to glaze over. It's now after midnight.

In the spirit of Monty Python's "just one thin mint", they brought us dessert. I can't remember what it was. Probably *tiramisu*. But that was just the warm-up. After we polished this off, we all jumped up to join the bride and groom out on the terrace, where their wedding cake and a massive boatload of fresh fruit were waiting for us. At least we were standing up at this point. More dancing followed. *Limoncello* and *Vin Santo* were offered but I was in need of an *amaro*, from the lovely family of *digestivi*, bitter and made from herbs, that aids in digestion.

We got home at 3:30 in the morning.

I love Nicola.

Whatever stereotypes you may hold in your mind about contractors - or about Sicilians - please discard them. Nicola Padrino, is one of only two Italians in this whole saga who has been 100% trustworthy, patient, sympathetic and brave. He has sacrificed for me and I have done the same for him. I would do anything for him and I believe he would do anything for me.

I have an occasional fantasy of what the script would look like if he and I were making a movie about this adventure-turned-disaster that we've been on for the past thirteen years. A lot of people have done me wrong. In the movie, I can picture myself asking Nicola to do me a favor. Someone needs to wake up with a horse's head in his bed. Alas, it's only a dream.

How did I get into this mess? Why couldn't I have accepted that my new life in retirement in Tuscany was going to be quiet and uneventful? Why did I take this risk by joining Lou in starting Anderò? The answer didn't take much analysis. In the second half of my life, I've become more of a risk-taker. Unimaginative early in my business career, I found myself becoming more adventurous in later years in business and in my personal life.

I analyzed the previous times in my life when I had taken a chance. Times where I could have taken the safe path and stayed put, but didn't. The vast majority of the risks I have taken have worked out beautifully for me and for Debbie. Now, perhaps to boost my confidence in this moment of self-doubt, I thought back to one of the biggest risks I took – leaving San Francisco for London in 1985.

Chapter 7 -- London? Why Me?

I remember it as if it were yesterday.

December 1984. Standing at my desk talking on the phone, I was gazing out at the Bay Bridge from two-thirds the way up 101 California Street, a sleek, glass office building near the Embarcadero in San Francisco. Kodak had just moved its San Francisco office from our historic building next to Ghirardelli Square and Fisherman's Wharf, overlooking Alcatraz, to this brand new Financial District high-rise. I was as happy as I could be. Life was great.

Four years earlier, after spending five years in San Francisco as a Sales Rep for Kodak's business products division, I had to make a decision to either stay in this most spectacular city or accept a move to Rochester, New York, Kodak's headquarters. It was impossible in those days to become a manager and move up the corporate ladder without accepting an assignment or two in Rochester at some point in your career progression.

Some people went there and never came out. I was not a "home office" guy but I knew I wanted more in my career. I had reluctantly left my apartment on Hyde Street, where the cable cars clanged past my front door every fifteen minutes, one block from Lombard Street, the Crookedest Street in the World, to spend two years in Rochester. I bought a condo overlooking Lake Canandaigua and did my duty so that senior management could look down upon me and judge whether or not I was management material. Those who did not make the grade usually begged to go back to the field as a Sales Rep, in order to escape the fish bowl culture that existed at Kodak's headquarters.

Something must have gone right because after

two years they gave me my first management assignment. On the same day that they announced my move, a friendly rival of mine a few cubicles away got the Sales Manager's job in New York City. I was crushed. To be in New York City, managing an aggressive sales team, would have been challenging and fun. Instead, I was going to the Western Region office near Los Angeles, not on the front lines, to manage a support staff. Not very rewarding and not many chances to shine was how I judged it. And it was in Southern California, which I had learned to look down upon with all my other friends in the San Francisco Bay Area who thought we were superior to the plastic, phony world of La La Land. "What's the difference between yoghurt and L.A.?" was on the front of a greeting card I once received. On the inside, it said, "One of them has live culture."

Every woman I met in L.A. seemed to be GU – Geographically Undesirable. You didn't date someone who lived ninety minutes away in stop-and-go traffic on the infamous Los

Angeles freeways. I spent hours every day commuting to and from a boring office.

After two years, I caught a break when the Sales Manager job opened up in San Francisco. I never thought I would get the chance to go back to my City by the Bay, so I was thrilled when I got the job. I was able to buy a beautiful house in the woods above Fairfax in Marin County, and I settled in. No more moves for me. Do a good job, help get my boss promoted so I could take her place as the District Manager for Northern California, and I would be happy for the rest of my life.

It was a good plan. I was eighteen months into it and my boss was a high flyer, so the chances of her moving onward and upward were good. I was single and straight in a city gay men were flocking to from all over America. Single straight women faced an undersupply of single straight men in the Bay Area. My dating odds were favorable. Life was good.

On that clear, beautiful December morning, I had no reason to believe anything could upset my plans for the future. My boss tapped me on the shoulder as I was on the phone. I turned and she gave me the "come here" gesture with her finger. I quickly ended my call and went into her office. She was on the phone and waved to me to shut the door. There was nothing to glean from her short replies to whomever she was talking to on the other end, as she hastily scribbled some notes. I sat down. She pushed a yellow Post-It note pad across the desk for me to read. It said

Kach ➜ London

I can still see that note and I picture her handwriting in my mind even to this day. WTF hadn't been invented yet as an expression, but looking back on it, that would have been my immediate reaction.

London? England? I was 36 years old and didn't have a passport. I was a Midwesterner from Ohio who graduated with a C+ average from Ohio University in 1970, where I spent four years playing basketball and cards, drinking beer, and studying every night for at least thirty minutes. My progression through college as I became more sophisticated consisted of moving through a series of card games in the dorm as we matured: Freshman year – Gin, Sophomore year – Hearts, Junior year – Euchre, Senior year – Bridge.

I majored in Business Administration because my mom and all of her friends were in Education and they all told me to run for the hills – there was no money in teaching. A stroke of luck had landed me a job with Eastman Kodak, at that time one of the most respected companies in the world; a company whose logo and trademark was in the Top 3 of the most recognized brands on the planet alongside Mercedes Benz and Coca-Cola.

I had several on-campus interviews with various companies in the spring of my senior year but had not received a single call for a second interview, let alone a job offer. Armed with my stellar C+ average, and a thorough knowledge of where all 33 bars were in Athens, Ohio, I had no idea what I was going to do when I graduated.

Kodak was one of my on-campus interviews and I had not heard back from them. One March evening, one of my friends announced he was getting married and the wedding would be back in his bride-to-be's hometown of Rochester, New York, in May. For one of the first times in my life I took some initiative. I wrote to Kodak, announced I was going to be in Rochester for a wedding the next month, and asked if I could please come to their home office for another interview.

The initiative paid off and the night before the wedding, while my friends and my brother from Toledo were partying, I found myself alone in my first posh hotel room near Kodak's head office. My interviews the next day went well and I was offered a job.

I was thrilled with the job and the company. They were so impressed with me, that after my 14-week training program, as my classmates were being assigned to Phoenix, Jacksonville and New York City, they sent me to Sioux City, Iowa, for my first sales territory experience. "What did I do wrong?" I asked the instructors. Their comment, "Don't worry, you'll be fine," didn't make me feel much better.

My likely career path, if I showed some promise in Sioux City, would have been a promotion to a sales territory in my district city of Omaha, and later on, assuming I could actually sell something, perhaps another sales territory in or around Chicago. In my two years in Sioux City I showed no such promise. But in my first of many career breaks, the significance of which I didn't realize until later, I heard they were looking for a sales rep who was single and who would be willing to be on the road for a year driving what we called the Kodak Microvan.

Our home office was looking for someone to tour the country selling a specialized microfilm check processing system to the banks. I jumped at the chance to get out of Sioux City and was pleasantly surprised when they picked me from a short list of other single sales reps looking for adventure. I said a tearful goodbye to my girlfriend and went off to

Rochester to be trained on the new system and pick up the Microvan.

It was a 28-foot long Winnebago camper that was painted in Kodak's iconic corporate colors and trademark. I would pull up in front of three or four banks per day and the local sales reps would bring their customers out to the van to sit through my slide presentation and demonstration of the equipment.

They built some hidden closet space for me in the back of the van to hang my polyester suits. I didn't sleep in the van, thank God. It was a year spent in hotels and motels, covering 45 states, where I got to meet most of the 250 sales reps and 35 District Sales Managers in the country. Giving four presentations a day for a year took me from a shy Sales Rep who was afraid to ask for the order, to someone who was gaining a reputation as an expert in the banking industry, and someone who was an excellent presenter. I was getting good press back in Rochester and I was loving it.

The highlight of the year was driving from

Cheyenne, Wyoming, to Spokane, Washington, over the course of a leisurely Labor Day weekend. I stopped in Yellowstone National Park and was thrilled as I watched Old Faithful go off a couple of times. Then I jumped back in the van and went about ten feet, whereupon the transmission went clunk and every gear was Neutral. They had to tow the van away and wait for parts to come in from Salt Lake City. There was a mass exodus of tourists that weekend as Labor Day meant school was about to begin, so I was pleasantly surprised when I walked up to the desk at the Old Faithful lodge and was told, "Yes, we have a room for you." I rented a car and laughed at how carefree it was to drive something less than 28 feet long as I enjoyed a splendid, peaceful weekend exploring this great national park.

At the end of the year, when it was time to turn the van over to my replacement, they gave me one of the most plum sales territories in the country: San Francisco, home of Bank of America and Wells Fargo Bank, the biggest players in an industry that bought millions of dollars of Kodak microfilm and equipment every year. It was a dream territory. From Sioux City to San Francisco in one year. I found my apartment on Hyde Street at the top of Russian Hill. I met my fellow Sales Reps after work every night at The Crow's Nest on Fisherman's Wharf, where we played Boss Dice to see who would pay for the Tanqueray on the rocks that we were all drinking.

My career path from 1970 to 1984 of Sioux City, to the Microvan, to San Francisco, to Rochester, to Los Angeles, and finally back to San Francisco flashed in front of my eyes as I sat there in my boss's office, staring at that Post-It note:

Kach ➜ London

She was still on the phone and my mind was racing. How could this be happening? I had never expressed interest in working outside the US. I didn't have a clue what Kodak did in London or the UK or Europe. I had heard about a couple of people in our division who worked internationally at Kodak, but they were guys who were sent on those assignments and were never heard from again.

She hung up the phone. "Why me?" I asked her. "I don't know," she said. "I'm as surprised as you are. Jack Lacy (the head of our division) has just picked you to do it."

She explained the job to me. Marketing Director for our division in EAMER (Europe, Africa and the Middle East Region). It sounded sexy. I would oversee training and marketing with a small staff supporting the 16 Western European countries, and liaise with Rochester to make sure products developed in the US were fit for purpose in Europe. It turned out to be the most enriching and rewarding job of my career. It would open me up to all the wonderful history and culture in Europe. And my home base was in London, where I was to meet my American wife. But one week before Christmas in 1984, sitting in Barbara's office, none of that was within my vision. As far from being worldly as you could get, it felt like they were asking me to move to

Mars. My heart was pounding as I left her office.

I had reluctantly given up my great life in San Francisco five years earlier and I had worked and maneuvered my way back just eighteen months ago, against the odds. I had a plan. Why were they messing with my plan?

My closest confident in our district was Sharon Zeller. Sharon was truly remarkable and she had the respect of everyone in the office. As one of the first female sales reps in Kodak's history in our division back in the middle 70s, she was brave, outspoken and smart. Whenever we brainstormed about ways to improve the business or win over a customer, it was usually Sharon's strategies that bubbled up to the top. She was never afraid to ask for the order. She was a leader, never a follower. She had vision. She was the first person I turned to a few hours later to tell her about the offer.

"I'm going to turn it down," I said.

"Oh, you can't do that," she said calmly, but

firmly.

"Why should I leave San Francisco?" I shouted. "I just fought my way back here eighteen months ago and have everything I want right here! Why are they doing this to me?"

She slowly talked me down off the ledge. She told me what a special opportunity this was for me; that London was one of the most exciting cities in the world; that I would grow in ways I could never imagine as a businessman and as a person.

"I would take it in a heartbeat if they offered it to me," she said.

I had asked for three days to make a decision. I got on the phone to the guy who was currently in the job and who was coming back to Rochester in an interesting, but not groundbreaking promotional move. He gave me a flavor of what it was like to work with our Kodak managers in the 16 countries and laid out the joys and challenges of the job. More encouragement from Sharon followed and as the third day approached I knew I could not turn this down. It would be taking me out of my comfort zone, but I finally began to see what a wonderful opportunity it was. "It will be a great adventure," I told myself. Just not the one I had planned.

Two weeks after Christmas, with my passport arriving at the last minute, I found myself on a British Airways flight from San Francisco to London for a meeting with all 16 Country Managers and to do some house-hunting for my permanent move in March. I was excited and apprehensive at the same time. I was about to go from comfortable, to having to learn about the cultures of 16 European countries and it frightened me just a bit.

I arrived at Heathrow airport on a bitterly cold Sunday morning, with snow swirling in the heavy wind. The General Manager for Europe had kindly sent his driver, Ron, to pick me up in the company Jaguar. As we drove to Covent Garden from the airport I was struck by how bleak and monotonous the architecture was outside London, as I struggled to understand Ron's east London accent from the back seat.

In 1985, Sundays were truly dead in London. Pubs and shops were closed by law. Theaters were dark. There was not a soul walking the streets around the hotel when Ron dropped me off, anxious to get home to watch his beloved Tottenham Hotspurs play on the telly.

Welcome to London, Jim. I thought of my home built into a forest of pine trees in Marin County, and of the deer I would frequently see while I relaxed in my redwood hot tub with friends. I asked myself, "What in the world have you done?"

As the years sped by, of course, everything would change. There was a woman to fall in love with, 16 countries to explore, a wedding, and more adventures in the US and England, before our path would lead us to Lucca in 2005. And to Anderò in 2007. Two years into my London assignment, I saw how narrow-minded I had been to want to stay in San Francisco. More than twenty years later, I know I made the right decision.

I met my Debbie in London about one year

after I arrived. She is an amazing woman. A lifelong educator who has written two books, she is an expert on Transition Education and has helped countless students, parents, teachers and schools to address the difficulty of transition and in particular, moving internationally. She is also a passionate advocate for developing intercultural understanding in children at a young age.

Our relationship was jump-started when, at a drinks party at a friend's home, she announced she was going to Greece for three weeks, but her best friend could only accompany her for the first two. Fuelled by a glass or two of wine, "I'll come join you for the third week," came tumbling out of my mouth.

We had only been on a couple of dates at that point and there had been a sizable gap between the first and second one due to our busy schedules. The others in our group just smiled at each other and I think I had another sip of wine. I was a bit surprised when she said, "That would be great!"

So a couple of months later, I found myself trying to fly from Seattle, Washington, where I was the best man in a great friend's wedding, to Skiathos, a Greek island in the Aegean Sea, via London and Athens. After the long, overnight flight from Seattle to London, I had a connection to Athens, where I had only one hour to change planes for the last leg to Skiathos. In the end, the tight connection didn't matter, as the flight I had booked from a notorious bucket shop in London (the name the Brits gave to cheap and cheerful travel agents) no longer existed, the schedule having been changed weeks earlier. So there was Debbie, golden brown after her first two weeks on the nearby island of Skopolos, waiting for me at the airport in Skiathos, but when she arrived, there was no flight and no Jim.

In 1986, my only way to communicate with Debbie was to call Maggie, her friend and flatmate, and ask her to relay messages to Debbie. Since Maggie was the one who had just spent the first two weeks in Greece with Debbie, she was fully sympathetic. Debbie might just have to face a third week on a sunny Greek island on her own.

With no flights until the next morning, and after being told they were sold out for the next two days, I found a cheap hotel in Athens for the night and took advantage of my first time in Greece to at least see the Acropolis and the Parthenon. I was in a bit of a dream-world as I sat at an outdoor restaurant underneath these wonders of the world, having just left rainy Seattle 24 hours earlier. I would try to get to Skiathos again in the morning but I didn't have much hope.

Back at the airport the next morning, my cultural learning continued with my discovery that there is no queuing in Greece. There were two people in front of a lone check-in desk, both vying for the clerk's attention. Behind them it was three across; then four abreast behind them. It was a flying wedge of about six people across at the back of the queue when I walked up, and judging by the level of shouting and the flailing of arms, I wasn't the only person who had been disappointed the night before.

Strategically thinking that I didn't stand a chance of elbowing a well-trained Greek out of position in the queue, I made a dash for the airline ticket office to plead my case. Lots of frowning, squinting, hesitating, and two-finger input on the computer keyboard ensued. Then she got on the phone. The flight was closing. This was hopeless. I had travelled more than 6,000 miles over a 24-hour period the day before and now I couldn't make the last 150 miles to spend a week on a sandy beach with the gorgeous Debbie. Chaos was all around me. I had already decided that if I didn't get on this flight, with the knowledge that the next few days' flights to Skiathos were fully booked, I would take a civilized British Airways plane back to London.

"Here!" the ticket agent yelled at me, shocking me out of my thoughts of sitting on the BA flight with a gin and tonic in my hand. "Take this to the check-in desk and she will give you a boarding pass. Hurry!" I sprinted through the terminal and was faced with a smaller, but still determined and emotional, wedge of people trying to get the lone check-in clerk's attention. I boldly adapted to the local culture.

"Here!" I shouted across the wedge, waving my magic piece of paper high in the air. "I'm supposed to get a boarding pass from you!" Bodies turned and faces stared at me. With an exasperated look, the check-in clerk waved me forward, slammed her rubber stamp down on a boarding pass and dismissed me with a wave of her hand. When I arrived breathlessly at the gate, I was pushed into the only unoccupied seat on a square-shaped WWII vintage plane that held about 20 people, all staring at me as if to say, "Where the hell have you been?" They slammed the door and we took off for the island of Skiathos. To this day I ask myself if would Debbie and I have still gotten married if I had taken the BA flight back to London.

The years between 1985 and 2005 were full of adventures and challenging new jobs for both Debbie and me, always with a happy ending. My career path from London onward was rich and varied and took us to a point in time when one day we could emotionally and financially make the decision to leave our jobs in London to move to Tuscany. For as much as we loved London, the pull of living in the little Tuscan gem called Lucca was too much to resist.

Chapter 8 -- Bella Lucca

Lucca is situated between Pisa and Florence in Northern Tuscany and therefore we have avoided the invasion of tourists that sometimes overwhelms our two more famous neighbors. Yes, we get busloads of German and French tourists on a daily basis in the summer, but they are day-trippers. They spend a half-day walking our flat, cobblestone streets, take their photos alongside the statue of Giacomo Puccini, our most famous citizen, and then they are off to fight the crowds in Florence; or to jostle each other trying to take pictures of the Leaning Tower of Pisa.

The result is that between 7:00 p.m. and 8:00 p.m. even in the summer, the streets are pleasantly busy, but not over-crowded, with a nice buzz of locals doing some last-minute shopping and having a Prosecco before going home to dinner. Then there is that transition that takes place in about a ten-minute period. You hear the metal gates of the shops on the Via Fillungo being pulled down for the night. Shop owners get on their bicycles and head for home to put a pot of water on the stove for pasta. A lovely sense of calm comes over every street. You see people walking to restaurants or to a bar for a Campari Spritz. The locals take the town back for themselves.

In my thirteen years here, I have seen a steady increase in tourism but never to the point where we feel overrun. The *New York Times* seems to be on a mission to tout our little bit of paradise every few months with articles about a new restaurant, or reminding everyone that we are at the heart of the operatic world of Tuscany. Foreigners come to stay in the many villas and farmhouses in the hills surrounding

Lucca for a week or two in the summer. They come into the city when they aren't at the beach or touring Chianti country and rent bicycles to ride around our famous walls.

Florence is what happens when you reach the tipping point with tourists. In any city where the tourists outnumber the locals, a strange phenomenon takes place. It no longer feels like a city – it feels like a theme park. It seems artificial.

I see it in the faces of the shop owners in Florence. The bigger stores are a bit too big to say *buongiorno* to anyone when you come and go. There is a coolness, a detachment in their demeanor when they wait on you. They seem to be thinking, "Just one more foreigner coming into my shop to buy something to tell their friends, 'I bought this in Florence'." In Lucca, it's just the opposite. The *buongiornos* you give and receive in every shop you enter are genuine. As you get to know the shop owners you strike up conversations with them and you get to know them on a personal level.

There are some wonderful Italian expressions, many of which show the good-hearted nature of most Italians. One of my favorites is *"piano, piano"*, which means "slowly, slowly". Italians can use it to show frustration with a bureaucracy that befuddles even them on occasion; to express exasperation at how long it can take to get things done. But it has a much more forgiving connotation when it is used in the context of learning the Italian language. In my first few years in Italy, here is the conversation that would ensue every time I walked into a shop to buy something.

Me: *"Buongiorno. Mi scusi, ma parlo solo un po d'Italiano."* Good morning, excuse me, but I only speak a little Italian.

Them: *"Buongiorno! No, parla bene!"* Good morning. No, it's not true. You speak well!

Me: *"Grazie ma non è vero. Sto studiando la lingua."* No, it's not true. I'm studying the language.

Them: *"Piano, piano!"*

Their *"piano, piano"* was giving me permission to learn their language at a leisurely pace, to make mistakes, to stumble over verb conjugations that I should have known already, and this little conversation always made our business transaction go more smoothly. They spoke to me in Italian, but more slowly and with compassion. I was grateful to every one of these lovely people each time they lied and said, *"No, parla bene!"*

For the first few years we lived here, people would tell us stories about how the Lucchese were aloof and closed to outsiders; how they didn't like tourists at all and would be just fine living in their enclosed magic kingdom inside the walls without any outside contact. That has changed noticeably over the years and the city has become much more tourist friendly. Perhaps the economic crisis that began in 2008 demonstrated that they needed a minimum level of tourism to survive. Now I see them reaching out more and promoting themselves in a more positive manner. And by the thousands, they are renting out their extra bedrooms, converted barns, and restored farmhouses to tourists.

The major attraction of Lucca is our wall. It's not just any wall. It's a wall with six million bricks in it. A wall so wide at the top that two lanes of cars used to drive around its circumference in the 1960s before they were banned. Four kilometers (2.5 miles) in circumference, it's a beautiful, flat surface on which to ride bikes, run, sit under a tree and most importantly, do the *passeggiata*.

The *passeggiata* is a walk but not just any walk. It takes place in the late afternoon or early evening, but it is especially noticeable on Sunday afternoons after the family has had their traditional Sunday lunch together. It is typical to see the grandparents walking with their children and grandchildren around the top of our famous wall. There are hundreds of them; the adults walking, the children on their bikes or in strollers. You'll also see some great-grandparents joining in, and it reminds me of one of things I love most about Italy. It's all about family and children. I have never seen a country more family oriented than Italy. When I see Nicola's arms tattooed with the names of his grandchildren, and I see him take them into his arms for a cuddle, it warms my heart.

You especially see this closeness in all of the family-owned businesses. Hardware stores, kitchen stores, restaurants, plumbers, electricians, builders... I could go on and on as I think about the people I come across on a daily basis where children and grandchildren have followed their parents and grandparents into the family business. This is a natural follow-on from another Italian phenomenon – children seldom move very far away from their parents.

I think about my life and how it was perfectly normal for me to leave my hometown at 18 years of age to go to university and then never to return to live there again. My career of moving every two or three years to another city for my job was accepted and expected in US culture. Not so in Italy or in other European countries. Home and family play a much more prominent role, sometimes to a comical excess. There is the famous story of a man who lived in Rome with his parents. He was 40 years old. The parents had finally had enough and they kicked him out of the house to live on his own. The man took his parents to court - and won. The parents had to take him back.

Some of this is no doubt related to economics. Italians are much more averse to borrowing money than in other countries. In America, if we can qualify for a mortgage, we grab it, and we grab as much as we can. During the lead-up to the financial crisis when lenders couldn't throw money at borrowers fast enough, you not only had the sub-prime mortgage problem, you had the additional risky and greedy practice of lending 100%, or more, of the appraised value of a home, assuming that property values would always go up, which exacerbated the crisis when they didn't.

Italians don't think that way. They hate paying interest. If you drive around the Lucca countryside you will see homes that are half-built and look like they are under construction,

until you go past them six months later and
nothing has changed. Italians are much more
likely to take €50,000 euros they have saved
and start building a house rather than going to
the bank for a mortgage. When the next
€50,000 comes along, perhaps a year or two
later, they build a little more. This goes on
until the house is built. They don't owe money
to anyone and they have not paid a euro in
interest. In the meantime they live at home,
where mamma cooks for them and does their
laundry. Even if they are 40 years old.

And it's not just Italy. Back when I was with
Kodak in London, I was working with the
French management team on how to improve
our business there. We were responsible for
product training and we had been especially
impressed with one of the French sales reps
who had come through training recently. We
did a little digging and found that he was one
of the stars of their sales team working and
living in the north of France.

We suggested to the head of our division in
France that he should transfer this guy to Paris.

He was clearly more valuable to them in Paris than he was in a small territory in the north of France. Our suggestion was met with a Gallic shrug and a "Go ahead and talk to him," response.

So I sent my American product manager to talk to this rising star and to convince him that the company, and his career, would be better served if he moved to Paris and took on more responsibility. The sales rep stared at him like we were asking him to learn Mandarin and move to Beijing.

"You don't understand. The town I live in is my home. The house where I live with my parents has been in our family for hundreds of years. Why would I want to leave that to move to Paris?" We clearly did not understand the cultural differences between the US and much of Europe. He stayed put.

I think of stories like that when I watch families enjoying each other's company on the *passeggiata* on Sunday afternoons. It makes me smile. They have their priorities in the right place.

A sense of calm and happiness comes over me when I enter *Centro Storico*, the historic center inside the walls of Lucca. In some ways it feels like a movie set, but in a quiet, understated way. It's the scale of the city that is so perfect. The streets are laid out in a Roman grid, with the two most important streets bisecting the interior. You can walk across the diameter of Lucca in twenty minutes from wall to wall. Or you can take the more leisurely path on top of the wall and pop down at the point closest to your destination. But as with any city where the borders are curved, the parallel street layout begins to meander and change as you walk the backstreets. I especially love the peace and quiet of these narrow lanes, especially in the middle of summer at the height of tourist season.

I never take a map into Lucca because it's fun to just wander and you can never get too lost. Keep walking and you'll find part of the wall at some point and get your bearings again. The small shops tucked away from the two main shopping streets are charming and they happily make a living without the benefit of a tourist ever walking past them.

Several large piazzas dominate Lucca. For me, the most beautiful is the *Piazza Napoleone* with a dozen plane trees framing the beautiful square facing the palazzo where Napoleon's sister lived and ruled in the early 1800s. When Napoleon arrived to take over Lucca and much of the surrounding area in 1799, there was no war. The Lucchese reluctantly let him in. He installed his sister, Elisa Bonaparte Baciocchi, as the Duchess of Lucca and she spent from 1805 to 1814 ruling Lucca from the grand palazzo that now houses local government offices, a museum, and the *Carabinieri*, the national police force. She did some good things in the areas of education and the arts but was still resented as a foreigner by the locals.

Her legacy lives on to this day as evidenced by her name still prominently displayed at *Porta Elisa*, one of the four main gates entering the city, *Via Elisa*, one of the two main streets

bisecting the city, and of course, *Bar Elisa*.
They couldn't resist.

Lucca's history is fascinating. Dating from the
11th century, the city was famous for its silk
trade and for negotiating its way out of
trouble. Threatened and ruled by both the
Medici from Florence and later by the Pisans,
Lucca's wealthy businessmen avoided wars
and somehow kept commerce going. The fact
that they felt they needed a wall so sturdy that
no one has ever breached it shows how serious
they were about protecting their independence.
There were four versions of the wall with the
first one built in Roman times. There were
later versions from the 11th and 13th centuries.
Finally, our magnificent Renaissance wall took
shape, so massive and so complex that it took
over one hundred years to build, from 1545 to
1650.

It's more than a wall. Eleven balustrades were
built as look-out points at strategic positions in
the wall, containing massive areas inside in
which to house troops and store munitions.
Just to make sure we were safe, a moat was

built around the entire city outside the wall. Lucca is built on a flood plain and that added to our security. After hundreds of years of trying to control the Serchio River, a dam upstream near the Devil's Bridge has finally ensured that Lucca today is free from flooding.

Within the walls, no buildings are higher than four storeys except for the churches and cathedrals. Ninety-nine of them. Yes, our walled city with a population of around 80,000 people, has 99 churches in it. Only a dozen or so are still consecrated and in use but that crazy number speaks volumes about this Catholic country where they would continually build monuments to their God and the Pope. I wish I had been present at the meeting back in the day when there were 98 churches in Lucca and someone stood up at a town council meeting and said, "You know what we need here? We need another church, that's what we need here!" I wish I could have heard that sales pitch. He must have been one hell of a salesman. Of course, it probably didn't happen that way at all. The Pope probably thought they were one church short of a full complement so he ordered another one built. And the people said, "Amen!"

Today the most famous use of the *Piazza Napoleone* is for the Lucca Summer Fest. More than a dozen artists come to Lucca during July to play at this intimate venue, which can hold no more than 10,000 people. We were really put on the concert map when the Rolling Stones chose Lucca as their only Italian stop on their European tour in 2017. When they went on sale, 55,000 tickets were gone in an instant.

But that isn't our biggest crowd of the year. Hundreds of thousands of geeks and freaks from all over Europe descend upon Lucca every year around Halloween for Lucca Comics and Games, the largest Comic-Con in Europe. The walls are transformed with giant marquees set up to sell the latest video games and other paraphernalia related to one super hero or another. We take our cameras and stroll the walls as thousands of visitors dress up as their favorite action hero, princess, zombie or literary character. It is Halloween on steroids. Funny how all my photos seem to be of Wonder Woman, and there are dozens from which to choose.

Giacomo Puccini is our most famous citizen and our opera house is a little jewel. Holding no more than 500 people but influenced by its more famous cousins like La Scala in Milan, we celebrate two or three of the maestro's most famous productions each year. *Tosca, Madame Butterfly, Turandot* – they all feature either here or at the amphitheater 45 minutes from Lucca at Torre del Lago, where he is interred in his summer house. One of the few musical geniuses of his era who became famous in his lifetime, he was noted for his expensive tastes, mahogany boats, cars, and for his many women. Oh, and for his smoking. In almost every photo you see of Puccini, he has a cigarette in his hand. Even the lovely bronze statue of him outside his museum in Lucca has him seated in a chair, holding a cigarette, as he gazes imperiously off into the distance.

He died in Brussels in 1924 while being treated for throat cancer.

I don't want to give you the impression that all is rosy and perfect in Lucca. There is that one small of issue of Italian drivers. It would be so easy for me to stereotype Italian drivers, but I refuse to stoop to that level. Not all Italian drivers are crazy. Only 20% of them are crazy.

This is not a scientific study, but in my many years of living here, my observations are that:

20% of Italian drivers drive far too fast.

20% of Italian drivers drive far too slow.

60% of Italian drivers drive moderately sensibly.

30% of Italian drivers have a total disregard of what painted lines on a road mean.

70% of Italians do not know they have turn signals.

80% of Italians have no problem speaking on their cell phone while driving. I have also seen Italians on bicycles going through a dangerous roundabout while texting.

90% of Italians do not know they have a rear view mirror.

If car manufacturers ever wised up to the fact that they could build cars for the Italian market without turn signals or rear view mirrors and never lose a single sale, they would save a fortune.

You math majors who are reading this are wanting to point out that my list adds up to more than 100%, so the obvious conclusions to draw from this are: a) many Italians fall into more than one of the categories above; and, b) math majors need to get a life.

In the thirteen years I have lived here, Lucca has been enthusiastically replacing traffic lights with roundabouts. Having also lived in England for thirteen years, I salute this effort. Roundabouts are infinitely more efficient at moving traffic and saving fuel. But local governments should do a feasibility study before rushing ahead, to see if the natives are equipped to take on these emerging technologies. The roundabout may be too advanced for some cultures. Some Italian drivers' behavior in roundabouts is a direct result of another trait most of them exhibit. They don't like to wait in a queue.

The proper way to navigate a roundabout is how they do it in Britain. You approach the roundabout and if no one is in the roundabout for at least the 180 degrees that you can see coming in your direction, you are free to proceed without stopping. Seems logical, doesn't it? We should use that logic in Italy too, shouldn't we? Oh, if it were only that simple.

The rule as applied in Italy is more primitive, actually. Well, it's not so much a rule as a philosophy. The Italian driver's philosophy is, "If I can get my car out in the roundabout before your car hits me, I'm good."

One day I was on my way to a meeting with my *commercialista* in *Centro Storico*. I had to navigate one particular roundabout in Lucca where you have to do a full 360-degree turn to come back to one of the few entrances in the wall where a car can enter. I use this roundabout frequently. I'm in the left-hand lane of our two lanes as I approach the roundabout. I have my indicator on, just for show. As I am making a full circuit of the roundabout, it requires me to be on the alert for not one, not two, but three streets coming into the roundabout from my right on my trek around. In Britain, you don't have to be "on the alert" once you are in the roundabout. Traffic at all three roads, in Britain, would be stopped, respectfully, behind their white line, awaiting their turn, as you would expect in a civilized society. But here in Lucca, I am about to face the most stressful ten seconds of my day.

Most of our roundabouts in the Lucca area are placed where two single-lane roads intersect. But this particular one has two lanes entering the roundabout from the four directions. This means there are six possible Italian drivers who are musing that, "I think I can pull out in front of him without getting hit," as I try to go around the circle as fast as possible in an effort to convince them to renounce their philosophy. I'm also going as fast as I can to try to intimidate them.

I try to make eye contact with them as I speed around the *giro*. I give them my best "Don't even think about it," look. But I know this is not enough. I must also be reading their eyes for the "I don't give a damn, I'm going" look coming back at me. Then it happens. One of them pulls out in front of me. I give him the horn. I scream, "It's not your turn!" It's not your turn!"

The other drivers waiting to test me have seen and heard all of this, and they wisely decide not to mess with me. I make it through the rest of the roundabout unscathed, feeling better now that I have taught one of them a lesson. My work here is done. I arrive at my meeting inside the walls *con calma*.

We have a few friends who own homes in the historic center. It is always a treat to visit them. Sitting in their apartments, you can't help but think of the families who preceded them. Renovations can't hide the fact that these buildings have stood for many hundreds of years. You can imagine the conversations that took place about what the Medici might do next. About the Pope. About what they thought Napoleon was up to.

For the first two years after we moved here in 2005, and with time on my hands, I would come to *Centro Storico* several times a week on my *motorino* to shop and have a gelato in the shade of the trees protecting the *Piazza Napoleone*. I was always impressed with the headquarters of the biggest banks, just one block away, with their prime locations facing one of the most beautiful churches in Lucca, in the *Piazza San Michele*. It is one of my favorite places inside the walls. The whimsical façade of the church, the friendly bars and gelato shops lining the streets, our favorite bakery around the corner; they all brought joy to my heart every time I was in town.

As the years passed, it was unfortunate that my love for this little section of town would slowly ebb away with every frustrating meeting we held at our bank's headquarters. The number of times I came out of the bank seething due to their incompetence, lack of authority, or just plain indifference was wearing me down. It ceased being a delightful piazza for me. From 2010 onward, our Anderò business was starting to suck the joy of life out of me.

Chapter 9 – Darker

As 2009 rolled into 2010, the reality started to sink in that the US financial meltdown was going to be more than a blip in what was a booming housing economy. Kevin the Rainmaker back in Toronto was having trouble getting anyone to listen to his sales pitch to invest in Tuscan real estate; therefore, no more money was going to come from Canadian investors.

Two of our outside investors put €150,000 into Anderò when we formed the company. One was a friend of Kevin the Rainmaker. The other one was Martin Prince, my boss and mentor from my last years working in London.

I have never met a man quite like Martin Prince. Quiet and unassuming, with no tell-tale signs of the massive ego that you see in many top business leaders, Martin has pulled off one business coup after another in his career. He spun a small photocopier company in the North of England into eventually running Kodak/Danka's $1 billion per year copier business in a dozen European countries. In the late 1990s, I was one of a dozen or so Senior VPs who reported to Martin after Danka had purchased the copier division of Kodak. He had my respect and the respect of everyone in the group. We knew we were in trusted hands as Danka began to implode in the US and in Europe.

In September of 1999, as the wheels were coming off the Danka/Kodak merger, Martin negotiated a nice leaving package for a half-dozen of his direct reports and we all moved on. We were a close-knit group and as we walked out the door together we pledged to stay in touch. Our paths would cross again and again as three of us ended up working for the same company years later and every two years around Ryder Cup time, we still gather with our wives for a long weekend of golf and reminiscing. More importantly, il Borghetto in San Gennaro would not exist if it weren't for Martin Prince.

We were desperate for more funding as we entered the construction phase, so we went to Martin with an offer. We would convert his €150,000 investment, which was unsecured, into a down payment on one of the apartments, in exchange for a loan of €400,000 so we could continue construction. While this offer meant that Martin would own equity by buying some bricks and mortar, instead of having his initial investment at risk, he did not have to make this loan. He knew the risks involved. If we couldn't finish construction and had nothing to sell, his €400,000 loan would be at risk. But he loaned us the money anyway. That's only one of the reasons why he is The Prince. It was the first of many times that I had to go to Martin in the ensuing years, hat in hand, asking either for additional funding or to ask him to buy one, and then two, and then eventually, three of the apartments so that we could finish the project. Each time that we met, I felt a mixture of embarrassment and failure as I had to explain how we were unable to pre-sell any of the apartments and that he was our only hope of moving the project forward. I so wanted him to respect me as a businessman and I felt that all hope of earning that respect was fleeting with each trip I had to make back to the UK.

He went from doing me a favor by investing €150,000 in Anderò, to owning more than half of il Borghetto. As he frequently reminded me, "I never wanted to buy real estate in Tuscany in the first place!" A man of great means, he already owned two large estates in the UK as well as a home in Granada and part of a home in Canada. The last thing he needed was another piece of real estate in another country. He was heavily involved in philanthropic efforts supporting children's schools in South Africa and he wanted to keep his life as simple as possible. I was adding complexity, and a touch of chaos at times, to his life.

This wasn't charity. He struck a good deal and we paid him a high rate of interest for his loan, but I always knew it was more the personal relationship that we had, and his compassion for the difficulties I was facing, that swayed his decision to help out time and again between 2009 and today. Il Borghetto would not exist if it weren't for The Prince.

Martin's loans got us through for a couple of more years when we had to shut down construction for the second time in 2012 as we had run out of money again. The project was 80% finished at this point. We were counting on selling one or two apartments during the building phase, which would have funded the rest of the construction. While that seemed like an easy task back in 2007, it was impossible now. The worldwide housing crisis was locked in and I was in despair as I saw no way we would be able to complete our half-built il Borghetto.

To add to my misery, money wasn't the only thing that had run out. Lou Codardo had skipped town.

When we last saw il Codardo, he was throwing the Mistress under the bus in Canada. She had told her husband she wanted a divorce and was going off to live with Lou in Italy. Too bad Lou wasn't following the same plan and he merely told his wife that he had seen the Mistress again and begged for mercy.

It wasn't too long after that when construction was shut down at il Borghetto, and we were trying to come up with a Plan B, that Lou said to me, "I've got to go back to Toronto for a bit to take care of some business."

"OK, when are you coming back?" I asked.

"In a few months. I have to come back to close on the house that I'm selling to the lawyer from Milan." I assumed we would then pick up the discussion of how we could finance the rest of the construction.

That was more than five years ago. I have not seen or heard from him since. Not a phone call. Not one e-mail with an insincere apology for having to stay home to mend fences. Nothing.

It was a pre-meditated getaway. He had stopped paying the mortgage on the house he was trying to sell to the lawyer. In the end, the lawyer outfoxed him by getting Lou to agree to let him move in and pay rent until they could sort out some legal issues with the house, created by our infamous *geometra*, Attilio Serpente. Then they would close the deal. At every step along the way the lawyer had lowered the price he was willing to pay and Lou could do nothing about it. Years later, after the bank finally foreclosed on the house, I'm certain the lawyer stepped in to pay off Lou's remaining loan and bought the house from the bank. He ended up paying less than half of the originally agreed price.

Lou was running away from much more. He had taken hundreds of thousands of euros from the Mistress in the past few years. First, he talked her into lending Anderò money, which when the troubles came, we were unable to pay back. Then he took more than a quarter of a million euros from her to build their dream home together. This was all during the period when he was checking the All of the Above box in his relationships with the Mistress and his wife. When il Codardo reneged on his promise to leave his wife, he and the Mistress had a villa under construction in the hills outside Lucca that was 90% complete and they didn't have the money to finish it. Or a relationship with which to continue. With that one-way flight back to Toronto, he was walking away from the banks and his two homes here, leaving the Mistress and me abandoned.

More significantly for me, he was running away from the company he asked us to start with him. He had no intention of putting a single euro more into Anderò to try to save il Borghetto. I ended up having to personally pay most of the Mistress's loan back to her when she sued Anderò. I don't blame her. Il

Codardo paid nothing.

Anderò Srl, which started out with three friends looking to have a good time, looking to make others happy by *Building Dreams in Tuscany*, and looking to make some money, had turned into a nightmare. I was left on my own to deal with the rubble as the reality of a non-existent real estate market came crashing down around me. I owed money to the banks, to The Prince, and to Nicola Padrino, our builder. Although not legally liable for their investment money, I felt a moral obligation to a couple of others here in Lucca who invested in us, and to some friends of Nicola down in Sicily. Under the Tuscan thumb had become my new reality. I became depressed as I thought about how the future might unfold, with The Prince losing all of his investment along with our other creditors, many of whom were friends. To say I felt like a failure was an understatement. My mind retreated to thinking about how I could have been smarter at each step along the way by making tougher decisions to stop the losses before they got out of hand. I had gone naively along for years thinking we could get out of this mess "if only….." The "if onlies" were never realistic and I should have known better.

Welcome to the golden years of retirement.

Chapter 10 -- Darkest

With il Borghetto 80% complete I had no money and no hope of finding more financing either through the banks or from The Prince to finish il Borghetto. All the banks by now had officially stopped giving mortgages to foreign buyers, which made our sales job even harder. I had an asset in il Borghetto, but only if it was finished.

I consulted a wise friend of my cousin Tom back in the States, who had made millions in business and as a restaurateur. I sent him all the gory details of the state of the business along with my financial position at the time.

He responded with, "You are not a wealthy man. This project will destroy you if you continue. Stop now and cut your losses. Walk away." While a little surprised at how bleak his message was, it was not a total surprise. I had always been naively optimistic throughout these past five years and had avoided taking a brutally hard look at the situation. Avoidance is not a trait I'm proud of, but it's there.

This was sound advice from someone who was not emotionally involved with the project or the people. This is what I needed to hear - a dispassionate third party who could give me rational financial advice. He made the case that this was beyond hope. Forget my emotions, he had told me, and run for the hills.

Yes, you're right. I didn't do that.

You would think that my head could overrule my heart in this situation. But it didn't. As I think back about my decision with my amateur psychologist hat on, and with the benefit of more than five years to reflect on it, here are the reasons why I couldn't walk away.

The Prince. I not only felt a moral obligation to him for the money he lent me but I also wanted his respect. If I did to Martin and the others what Lou had done and just walked away, I would be a coward just like he was. I had to fight to try to get as much of Martin's investment in Anderò, which was an investment in me, back to him. Taking his money, and then throwing in the towel and taking the easy way out, was unacceptable to me.

Il Padrino. It can bring me to tears to think about what a great friend Nicola has been and how he has put himself at personal and professional risk by sticking by my side when he knew I could not continue to pay him. Of all the Italian characters in my life story, it is the Sicilian builder who has shown more grace, more loyalty and more honesty than any of the others. If I let him down, I would be letting down his extended family as well. I couldn't do that.

Giulio and his friend. Years ago when we were desperate for investors, Lou strong-armed Giulio, the owner of a custom-kitchen business and the man who built la Casa Gialla, to invest €50,000 with Anderò, in exchange for a promise that we would use his company to put in the six kitchens at il Borghetto. The father of Giulio's right-hand man also came in for €50,000. These were unsecured investments. They would get their money back plus a profit only if Anderò were profitable. This was more than just a loan from a supplier. Giulio was a friend.

Our Canadian buyers. Like Martin, they had first invested in Anderò and later turned that investment into a down-payment on an apartment. They would be left out in the cold as well if we didn't finish the project.

These were the people I would be letting down if I walked away now. I couldn't do it.

I needed to pump more money into il Borghetto and my options were becoming limited. Many years earlier, when I was flush with cash, I had helped my brother out when he needed to sell his home back in the States. I bought it from him so he and his wife could continue to live there. I felt terrible now when I had to pick up the phone and tell them that I needed to sell the house. Disrupting their lives for a year as they shed a lot of their furnishings to move into a smaller home added another layer of guilt and embarrassment to the personal pile of rubble I was building.

The money from that sale got our construction going again but I knew it wasn't going to be enough. I procrastinated as long as I could before facing the fact that if I were to finish il Borghetto, I would have to sell our home in London. The day I broke that news to Debbie was one of the hardest days of my life.

Owning a home is fairly dispassionate for me. I saw our house in London as our pension fund and income generator, but for Debbie, it was also her emotional link to England. She often spoke of how she always wanted to own something there, even if it was a small apartment, to know that we could always go back if we wanted. Now I was trampling on that dream. Debbie didn't try to fight the decision as once again she placed her trust in me. But the cool silence of the next few days and the sadness that I saw in her eyes gave me one more reason to feel guilty. I was wrong to think this was a one-off business decision that I could put behind me once it was made. It turned out to be much more than a financial decision and the emotional scars are still with me today.

Ignoring the advice of the friend who had told me to run for the hills, I flew back to London and broke the news to my renters, who had been in place for eight years and were dream tenants, that I could not renew their lease. I put some money into sprucing up the garden, one of the house's greatest assets, and listed it with the agent who sold it to us. We didn't even have to put it on the market, as there had been a family who had just been gazumped (the quaint British practice of having another buyer outbid you even after you have agreed a price with the seller) on another home on our very road. They offered me 98% of my asking price. I told them I couldn't possibly accept the offer, as we hadn't even put it on the market or sent out the glossy brochure. The next day they agreed to my asking price.

At this point, I was only focused on closing on the sale so I could put the money into Nicola's hands to finish the construction. Martin Prince came to the rescue once more, giving me a bridge loan so we didn't lose more valuable time. In the back of my mind I was afraid that Martin was thinking that I was using him as my personal ATM with each emerging crisis. I just wanted the crises to end. My hope was that with a completed il Borghetto, we could sell the apartments and I could at least make Martin whole. Painfully and belatedly, I was coming to the realization that even if we sold all of the apartments, the anchor around my neck of our other project, la Porcellaia, would mean that I wouldn't be able to pay back any of the other investors who had put their trust in me. As that reality sunk in, my depression deepened.

Most all of the money from the sale of our house in London went to Nicola Padrino, who was standing by, ready to throw his Sicilian team into the final 20% of construction needed to finish il Borghetto. In late spring of 2014, seven years after we formed Anderò Srl, we finished the beautiful six apartment complex, complete with a lovely 15 x 60 foot swimming pool, with views up to the historic village of San Gennaro and down the valley toward Lucca. Without much landscaping and with none of the apartments furnished, there was no "wow" factor for me as I looked upon our completed project. There were only feelings of pride at having crawled across the finishing line – and a tightness in my stomach at the reality that this beautiful building solved none of my financial problems.

I had risked all that I had to finish the construction and we finally got our occupancy permit in July of 2014. Our Canadian friends and Martin Prince had been waiting for more than five years to close on the apartments they had agreed to buy. "Please take our money so we can legally own our apartments," they had pleaded many times. So naturally, it was time for the bank to screw me over one last time.

Once we had our occupancy permit, the bank's task was very simple. They had to take our €600,000 construction loan, which was for the entire project, and divide it between the six apartments. Easy peasy, as the British would say. Then, at the closing in front of the *notaio*, the amount assigned to each apartment would be repaid for each of the five units that had been sold at that point.

Seven months later, we still had not closed a single sale as Martin and the Canadian buyer sat and stewed. It took the bank from August until late November to send us a letter saying the fractionalization of the loan to the individual apartments was now in place. They said this decision was valid until the end of January, when for some reason, it would expire and the bank would have to reevaluate the numbers if we hadn't sold the units by then.

No problem. We had buyers at the ready.

Avanti!

The next step was for the bank to draw up the legal descriptions, loan amounts, and other details to send off to the *notaio*, so he could orchestrate the closing. The bank said this would take one month. It was the beginning of December 2014 when they said that.

From December 15th through the end of the year, I could hardly find anyone working in our bank. Holiday season was upon us. Just like in August, when it is almost impossible to do any serious business in Italy because most Italians are on holiday on the island of Sardinia, the Christmas holiday season slows everything to a halt and it doesn't end on New Year's Eve. We have *La Befana*.

There are not many countries that have more religious holidays than Italy. So many saints - so few days. The tradition of *La Befana* lives throughout Italy today, connected to the Epiphany on the 6th of January, a national holiday. It originated as a Christian legend, but now she exists as a mythical woman on a broomstick who flies around giving candy to the children (if they have been good) on the Eve of Epiphany. If you go to a restaurant on the night of *La Befana*, you are bound to be entertained several times during the evening by women dressed up as witches as they run through the restaurant cackling and handing out candy to delighted children. That means that no one goes back to school, or gives any thought to serious work, until well after January 6th each year.

The bank missed the January 31st deadline. I was furious.

When I asked them why it took so long from our August occupancy permit to the November agreement on how to fractionalize the construction loan, the answer was, "We only have two guys in Rome who make these decisions; and there are hundreds of file folders sitting in their in-basket at any one time."

Piano, piano my ass. I'm getting screwed here.

Do you think the bank could say, "I'm sorry

we missed the deadline? Here are the documents you need for the closing. Let's go ahead." They could not. Because they had missed the January 31st deadline, all the documents went back to these two sad souls in Rome, to sit at the bottom of their in-basket again.

Finally, in early spring, a new letter was dispatched from Rome. I pictured white smoke coming from their chimney with each new decision they made. It happens with about the same frequency as electing a new Pope. The terms and conditions and assigning the €600,000 to the six apartments was exactly the same. They just gave us a new date when it would all expire again.

The bank finally got their act together and sent the documents to the *notaio*. On a bright spring day in 2015, we officially sold the five apartments, eight years after Lou, Raul and I sat down to form Anderò Srl. The Tuscan thumb attached to my bank had cost me thousands of euros in interest that I had to pay during the delay from our occupancy permit to the day we were able to record the sale of the apartments. I spoke with my lawyer about suing them to recover the money I lost due to their incompetence. "Yes, you would win this case," he said. "It will take at least six years in the courts. I suggest you drop it." That feeling of not knowing whether to laugh or cry on the day we sold five apartments was mixed with anger as well, as I had lost count of the number of times the bank had screwed me over in the past eight years.

You might be wondering how Debbie was reacting to all this turmoil. To her great credit, she has never blamed me for the mess I have gotten us into. She questioned my judgment in choosing to go into business with a character like Lou, and rightfully so. She has sacrificed during our thirty years of marriage by accepting my corporate moves to support me in my career, and she has been grateful for the wonderful opportunities we have had in our married life. Now that times are difficult she is still here supporting me, and my love for her seems inadequate for all that she has endured.

In those dark years between 2011 and 2015, my emotional state alternated between denial fueled by naïve hope, and depression based on reality. I felt helpless as I burned through my remaining assets to finish il Borghetto, knowing that it was close to impossible to find outside buyers for the apartments. There was only one piece of joy I had in my life outside Anderò. One place I could escape to for a few hours once a week and forget completely about the latest crisis. Combined with the close friendship of a few steadfast friends, the golf course was my escape.

Chapter 11 – Golf and the Commercialista

I have a great *commercialista*. Vittorio Campione. Not only a great accountant, but a great friend as well. He and I have become golf buddies and not a week goes by in the summer when we are not at the beautiful Montecatini Golf Club in the hills outside this famous spa town, thirty minutes from Lucca. It's not the most posh golf course in the world because they don't have much money to keep it in great condition, but it is one of the prettiest golf courses you will ever see.

They built the course in the middle of olive groves and vineyards high in the rolling hills. They left hundreds of olive trees dotted around the course, just to mess with you. There is one guarding the front of the green on the opening hole. There are also cherry trees, plum trees and pear trees scattered around. We will be driving the golf cart down the 14th fairway and Vittorio will veer off to the right side of the fairway. *"Attenzione! La mia pallina è sinistra!"*, I tell him. Hey, my ball's over there on the left. He ignores me, screeches to a halt, jumps out and starts picking plums, which he consumes on the spot.

Golf is quite expensive in Italy and it is not wildly popular. Most of the golf courses struggle financially and they depend on tourists during the summer season to make ends meet. This means the courses are rarely crowded and that makes it a special treat. We call it Champagne Golf. We walk down the fairway in perfect weather with a view of San Miniato, famous for its summer truffle festival, the Lucca plain and the Pisa mountains off in the distance, with no one pushing us and no one holding us up.

On many golf courses in America, the marshall chases you around in his cart, pushing you to speed up play. After nine holes, you grab a hot dog at the clubhouse and eat it in the cart so you don't lose your place. God forbid those bastards behind you, who made some rude comments about how long it took you to find your ball on the 5th hole, should jump ahead of you at the turn. Screw them.

At Montecatini, we tee off at 11:00 a.m. and play the front nine. Then we park the cart and go up to the terrace of the old stone clubhouse, featuring an entire wall taken over by a purple flowering bougainvillea. It's a proper restaurant. Not a hot dog in sight. We have *spaghetti con olio, aglio, pepperoncino e parmesan* - and a beer. Or perhaps *le penne arrabbiata*. We tally up the front nine and the winner does some trash talking. Then we are off to play the back nine with perhaps only one other group, who has also stopped for lunch, to negotiate with as to who goes off first on the 10th tee. It is so civilized. No one paid the bill when we got up from lunch because the restaurant knows that it's the loser after 18 holes who has to pay.

Montecatini's signature hole is the Par 3 18th. 140 meters long (154 yards), all carry across a big pond from an elevated tee. The clubhouse is framed behind the green and in the distance are forested mountains with villas perched here and there. It's one of my favorite spots to stand in all of Tuscany. The thrill of coming to this hole with a match still on the line makes my day.

There are small, sponsored tournaments almost every weekend in the summer. Last year, Vittorio and I decided to enter one sponsored by *Rigoni di Asiago*, a major Italian maker of *marmellata* (jam), *miele* (honey) and *Nocciolata* (a chocolate and hazelnut spread similar to Nutella).

A two-ball, better ball competition with Stableford scoring, Vittorio and I seemed to click, as when one of us had a bad hole, the other one came through with a good hole. Damn if we didn't win the event and an hour after the tournament was over, we were called up to the presentation tent and given a lovely wooden box with a selection of six *Rigoni* products inside, along with six silver tasting spoons. Even better, they told us that we had now qualified for the regional semi-finals, to be played at the famous *Poggio dei Medici* course outside Florence later that summer.

Vittorio is a serious golfer. Not pretty to watch, but he has a determination and a grittiness around the greens that frequently has him scoring better than you would think he is capable. He insisted that we go to *Poggio dei Medici* on our own a couple of weeks before the semi-finals so we could scout the course.

The day of the semi-finals arrived and right from the start we were playing like we did back at Montecatini. On the par 4 first hole, Vittorio's tee shot was wide right and his next two barely stayed in bounds. He finally arrived on the green with his fourth shot. In the meantime, I had hit a decent drive but had a completely blind shot for my second as the hole was down a steep hill with a tree dead-center in the middle of the fairway blocking my way. Why do the Italians do this? I hit a good shot but had no idea how it ended up

until we got to the green and saw my ball 15
feet from the hole. I missed the birdie putt
(hey, I have a 13-handicap for a reason) but our
par got us off and running. I propped up the
team on the first half-dozen holes and then
Vittorio came into form. He parred the final
three holes, including getting up and down
from a bunker 30 yards short of the green on
the closing hole. We posted 41 points and
waited to see the results.

Damn! We won again!

Now we're really laughing. More jam. More
Nocciolata. More photos with the winners of
the other categories. And I kept asking
Vittorio, "Why didn't you sign us up for a
tournament with Armani as the sponsor? I
don't need any more jam. I need an Armani
sport coat!"

Then the big surprise. Our victory entitled us
to an all–expenses-paid weekend at a lovely
golf course and spa hotel called Argentario in
Southern Tuscany for the National Finals,
spouses included. We had a great time and got

to play a practice round the day before the tournament, except for the 18th hole. It was closed because the famous Italian director, Paolo Sorrentino, was shooting a movie about Berlusconi called *Loro*, and they had taken over the hotel and grounds for a couple of months. We had to dance around the production company more than once during the weekend. We didn't worry about not seeing the final hole. We were ready.

The next day we played well again and stood on the 18th tee with 41 points, the same number that had won us the regional semi-finals. You don't know how the other teams are doing, so you just go for as many points as possible. The 18th was a crazy par 4 with two different fairways to choose from and two small slots to get to the main part of the fairway for your approach shot to the green. Not being able to play the hole the day before doomed us. We both botched the hole completely, with Vittorio picking up his ball, and me missing a three-foot putt that would have given us our 42nd point.

That night at the lavish banquet they handed out the prizes. We were shocked when they called out our names for finishing second. You guessed it; more jam, more Nocciolata, more photos. We were still giggling when we got back to our seats and they announced the winners, also with 41 points! We had tied for first. In these tournaments there is no playoff. They do a count-back and in this case the team that had the better score on the second nine holes was declared the winner.

We were crushed. My missed three-footer on the 18th cost us the tournament, a National Championship of sorts. Vittorio tried to hide his disappointment but we both spent the rest of the weekend reviewing our hole-by-hole performance and saying to ourselves "if only....".

I apologize to all you non-golfers who have had to slog through this story, Debbie included. And to all you golfers, I know you feel my pain.

Vittorio's comportment on the golf course

mirrors his work as my accountant. He is honest to a fault. "Creative accounting" is not a term he understands. He follows every bureaucratic twist and turn in Italian fiscal law to the letter. There is a double-thick, encyclopedic book that is published by the government every year with all the latest rules for accountants. Then during the year, he has to keep up with the modifications that come out of Rome on a regular basis. If a decision had to be made by the officers of Anderò Srl, Vittorio made sure to create and have me sign the three necessary letters: one calling for a meeting; one stating the meeting took place; and a third detailing what decision was taken at the meeting. The fact that no meetings ever took place and I was the sole decision-maker was irrelevant. We were following the rules.

He is tough and he has my back. When our finances became a mess and we were fighting with the bank, Vittorio led the charge. He took great pleasure in pointing out to them when they had screwed up. He tried to pressure them to do the right thing. He wrote letters to

the bank's headquarters in Rome. He was
diligent. He has been a great mentor to me in
plotting our strategy moving forward. On
more than one occasion I have received a text
from him in the middle of the night on some
small detail of our Anderò business because he
couldn't sleep. He's a star and I love him
dearly.

Chapter 12 – Moving Forward

As if my financial problems with Anderò weren't bad enough, I was frequently reminded of, and frustrated by, what I call the Stupid Tax. When I did my T-chart back in 2005, predicting that it would be 40% less expensive to live in Italy compared to living in London, I had no column in my spreadsheet for the Stupid Tax. But I should have. This is the category for all those little things that cost you money after you move to another country because you haven't yet learned the system. That €100 ticket you received in the mail after your first excursion to Florence, for driving past a ZTL sign? Stupid Tax. How about driving around the block and going past the ZTL sign a second time in ten minutes? €200 – Stupid Tax. The *Zona Traffico Limitato* system is common now, but was new to us in 2005 when we moved here. To keep all traffic except residents out of certain neighborhoods, cameras are placed just after the ZTL sign warning you that you are about to enter a restricted area. If you pass the camera, your license plate is captured and months later you get a surprise in your mail box. Now we know.

We never received a bill for rubbish removal after we moved in. They didn't pick up rubbish at your house in those days. Bins for recycling and rubbish were sporadically placed alongside the road (ours was almost a mile away) and you dropped your rubbish off on your way down the hill to the main road. I assumed this was included in our small property tax bill that we paid each year. Wrong. After several years when I finally found out that we had to pay separately for rubbish removal and that we had to go to the central office to register, I found that we owed €1,000 for our back payments. Then there was a fine on top of that for not paying. Another €1,000. What? The fine is 100% of what you owe? I took the bulldog, Vittorio, with me to negotiate with them as I was convinced I was being given a 100% penalty simply because I was a *straniero*. Not the case we were assured. The rule is the same for everyone. We never received a bill from them or a warning that we were in default. But we were clearly in their system as they pulled up our address on their computer and knew what we owed to the penny. It makes me wonder what would have happened if I had never gone into their office. Would they have just sat there for another 20 years with my bill of say, €10,000 plus a penalty of €10,000 on their books? At what point would they have cared? The €1,000 penalty I paid goes in the Stupid Tax column.

Paying a penalty for forgetting to go to the automobile registration office annually to pay your car tax? Stupid Tax. Like the rubbish removal folks, they don't send you a bill either.

Dozens of other little expenses, such as all the fees you pay for the privilege of having a checking account at the bank, fall into the category that I forgot to include in my analysis of how inexpensive it was going to be to live in Italy. Stupid Taxes. Stupid me.

As annoying as these little things were to me, I had bigger problems. The worldwide economic crisis deepened between 2008 and 2012, and a strange phenomenon occurred here in Tuscany regarding selling homes to foreign buyers, which was our target market. A few locals were selling their properties for significantly lower prices. But most of them didn't lower their price -- they just waited. This fact combined with basic economics created a nightmare scenario. In basic economic terms, if you have a market with an equal number of buyers and sellers you are likely to see stable prices. When a market gets imbalanced with, for instance, 60% sellers and 40% buyers you are likely to see prices fall. And prices will rise if there are more buyers than sellers. Simple economics.

But those rules don't apply when the imbalance becomes too great. When il Borghetto was nearly completed in 2013, I showed the project to the real estate agent who had sold us the abandoned farmhouse back in 2007. She was impressed with the quality of construction, the finishing touches, everything about it. She was also depressed, as was every other real estate agent in Lucca, because we were now in year five of the deep economic recession and they had sold very few properties in the past couple of years.

"So how much are you asking?" she said.

"€325,000 for each of the two bedroom, two bathroom apartments," I said.

"Oh, that price is too high. There are several other projects with apartments like yours, also with a swimming pool, that are for sale for €250,000 to €275,000. They are not as nice as yours, but you are overpriced."

Typical real estate agent, I thought. Looking to

beat down the price to make her job easier.

I thought about our conversation for a few days and then I wrote to her and said, "So if I were desperate to sell the apartments at il Borghetto, and I lowered the price to €200,000 per apartment, I assume you could move all of them within six months or so." That is what would happen in a normal market where there was an imbalance with more sellers than buyers. Her reply was chilling.

"Well, no, I probably couldn't sell any of them because we don't have any buyers at the moment," she said.

I wrote back, "Well then, we don't have a price problem, do we? We have a 'no buyers' problem." I told her that in my opinion the market imbalance was so bad that it felt like our local market was 90% sellers and 10% buyers. Her reply was even more unsettling.

"More like 95%/5%, I would say. I apologize. You are right. You don't have a price problem."

So all the local real estate agents who had been telling me "Your price is too high," were just hiding the fact that they didn't have any foreign buyers - at any price. The worldwide economic crash born in the USA had now officially paralyzed the previously recession-proof, holiday-home property market in Tuscany.

The Prince and I discussed the challenges we faced. We agreed that the sales market would take years to recover. Our job was to take advantage of the fact that we had an asset that was fully built and beautiful.

There was one thing that was actually working in our favor. Everyone still loves coming to Tuscany for a holiday, even in a recession. If sales are out – rentals are in. Our strategy became, "Let's ride out the recession by launching ourselves as a premier villa in the holiday home rental market." We set out to furnish the first couple of apartments and test our ability to attract foreigners to our little Borghetto in the hills below San Gennaro. We put money into landscaping and other improvements to give it the "wow" factor that it has today. Cypress trees lining the curved entrance, stone steps leading up to the pool, and beautiful hedges of photinia and bay laurel surrounding the property, are the first things our guests see after they arrive at our gated entrance. My spirits lift as we transform il Borghetto from just a beautiful building to a warm and inviting holiday home.

After seven grueling years, we had built a beautiful Italian home, loaded with charm, comprising six apartments built with some of the finest Tuscan touches. We combined chestnut beams and handmade terracotta tile floors with modern conveniences like in-floor heating. The quality was superb and Nicola Padrino was duly proud. We would frequently walk through the apartments and he would run his hand over a particularly well-built curved wall in a bedroom, put there to accommodate the space needed for the shower in the bathroom on the other side. We patted the massive chestnut beams that were laid so carefully, that years after the construction was completed, there were no signs of settling cracks anywhere. Our Sicilian builders are true craftsmen.

Because we were given the exact square meters and cubic meters to work with as were in the original building, and no more, we made the most out of every nook and cranny. Not only are no two apartments alike – there are no two rooms that are the same. Every bedroom, every bathroom is unique.

Each apartment has its own character, like Casa Pinocchio. This apartment has a high cathedral ceiling and because there was a faint outline of a double door from hundreds of years ago in the original building, we were allowed to install a massive double-wide, glass front door.

A year or two after il Borghetto was finished, I met 90-year-old Signore Bianchi. He was the last occupant of our property and when he was a small boy he lived above the room with the cathedral ceiling. He explained to me why it was shaped that way. This room was the barn

for the donkeys; that's why there was a barely
visible outline of a brick double door in the
original building. He said they had an old
donkey and a young donkey. When the old
donkey died they got a younger one. They
pulled water from the stream 25 meters away
as the well in front of il Borghetto hadn't been
dug yet. As he sat in our modern rocking chair
in the bedroom where he grew up, I couldn't
help thinking about all the other Bianchis who
had lived at il Borghetto in the hundreds of
years before he came along. I am always
conscious of the history of our great building
and I'm proud that we used as much of the
stone and bricks from the original farmhouse
as we could when we brought Il Borghetto
back to life. To think that most of the stone in
il Borghetto could be part of two structures on
the same spot for 800 years or more is inspiring
to me and increases my love of what we
accomplished.

With no sales prospects in sight for the
apartments, we started our holiday home
rental business in 2014. Who wouldn't want to

come rent one of our apartments for a week or two in the summer? This should be easy. Finally, we might be catching a break.

If you go to VRBO/HomeAway and search for a vacation rental in Tuscany, do you know how many hits you will get? As I write this, the number is over 50,000. That's my competition – 50,000 other apartments, villas, and farmhouses, all promising a bit of summer fun under the Tuscan sun. Yikes!

"OK, calm down," I tell myself. "That's not really my market. Surely my market is for people who want to see Lucca and be close to Florence and Pisa, who want to be in the country, in a peaceful setting with a swimming pool." So I search for holiday homes in Lucca province with a swimming pool. That should narrow it down, eh? Another yikes! Still more than 1,000 hits. How are people ever going to find us?

With a little research I discover there aren't really 1,000 swimming pools at homes for rent in Lucca province. That number reflects the fact that many places like ours have multiple apartments for rent. Somehow this doesn't make me feel any better. The competition is fierce and every farmer and his *moglie* (wife) with a spare room seem to have discovered how to market it on the Internet.

We offered our first two apartments to the world in April of 2014. It wasn't until a year or two later that I discovered that about 75% of our guests book their summer holidays in January, February, and March. We had a few weeks of rentals that first year in spite of the competition and the fact that we had no guest reviews to spread the word on the beauty of il Borghetto. In this business it is all about getting the word out and getting positive reviews from your guests.

I loved making sure our guests were happy: welcome baskets of food so they could have a nice pasta lunch or dinner if they hadn't yet been to the store; pre-booked entry times for them in Florence so they didn't have to stand in line to see the David; sending them to the best restaurants and wineries; even taking them to our beautiful hillside golf course in Montecatini; it was all part of the service. Our early guests wrote glowing reviews.

In our second year we broke through and had about 20 weeks of rentals in our two apartments and we were adding five-star reviews to the website after almost every stay. The Prince, who saw the potential of our rental business and who always looks at the big picture, had stepped in to buy additional apartments so we could add them to the rental pool.

In 2016 we had four apartments in the program and the following year we put the fifth apartment into rental, all thanks to The Prince. Our revenues grew by 60% in 2016 and a further 45% in 2017.

There is another big reason why il Borghetto is so beautiful today and I do mean big. Domenico Grande and his wife, Nadia, are the caretakers of our lovely property. Domenico is one of the family members who came to Tuscany with Nicola and company all those years ago to build a new life here. He is a giant of a man in more ways than one. He was part of the crew who helped shape il Borghetto in every sense of the word. Domenico is a magician with an excavator.

Early on in the construction, Nicola and Domenico decided that to give il Borghetto stability and a proper platform for the foundation, they would build a wall one-and-a-half meters high and 30 meters long behind the main building. Domenico went to work moving truckloads of dirt and debris to give the property its initial profile; then did his part by helping to lay the stones for the spectacular, curved wall. He similarly shaped the area surrounding the swimming pool to give us a graceful path from the main building to the pool.

When the construction was nearly finished, Domenico approached me and asked to stay on as our caretaker. I quickly discovered the main reason why – he loved il Borghetto as much as I did. His emotional attachment to the project is amazing. He doesn't just cut the grass and clean the pool. Not a week goes by when he isn't whispering in my ear, suggesting a row of box hedges here, or better lighting there, to make our property even more beautiful. Every one of his suggestions is spot-on and I always wish I had thought of them first.

I'm amazed that his *buon occhio* also extends to landscaping. How can he be so rough and rugged, able to move impossibly heavy boulders with his bare hands one minute, while the next minute extolling the virtues of using photinia instead of bay laurel in a new hedge? His endurance is impressive. He works a full week for Nicola and then comes to il Borghetto at night and on weekends to make sure every olive tree is manicured and every one of our six new cypress trees is watered. In the summer, it is not uncommon to get a text from him at 10:00 p.m. as he is finishing cleaning the pool, reminding me that he and Nadia will be there bright and early the next morning to clean-the apartments for that day's arrivals.

Nadia is a sweetheart, working with me on

Saturdays when we have multiple departures
and arrivals to make sure the apartments are
spotless and the *Prosecco* is in the fridge. Both
of them are always looking for new ways to
make our guests happy. Domenico introduced
me to the local butcher in his village. When the
Sicilians arrived years ago they gave the
butcher their secret recipe for *salsiccia piccante
Siciliana* (spicy Sicilian sausage) and with one
day's notice, the butcher will produce two or
three pounds of this wonderful treat. For our
special guests at il Borghetto we offer a catered
barbecue dinner with Domenico and Nadia
firing up our charcoal grills to produce *Bistecca
Fiorentina*, ribs, chicken, and the *salsiccia* for our
guests while I make the *cannellini* bean salad
and *torta di mandorle, limone e ricotta*. It is a
feast to remember. On Saturday nights when
the lawns have been mowed and il Borghetto
sparkles, I revel in the sound of children's
laughter coming from the pool as they sneak in
one last swim before dinner. While I had many
successful moments in the business world, the
level of satisfaction that comes from making
people happy at il Borghetto brings a special

joy to my heart.

We had finally stopped the bleeding and bought ourselves some time. We have a rental business that is thriving and returning some annual income to the owners. Il Borghetto is now a fabulous asset. We can continue to grow our holiday home-rental business in the coming years until the time some of our summer guests might want to buy one of these apartments for their own. The repeat business that we have had from clients from one summer to the next has convinced me that this is a likely source of our future buyers. Either that, or an investor will come along who will want to buy the entire project and live off the rental income.

From 2015 onward, I felt myself relax a bit. Our personal financial situation was still dire but at least we had stopped the heavy outflow of cash to support il Borghetto, and I felt a bit of relief that I didn't have to go back to Martin Prince in a panic to ask him to save my ass once more. I can breathe again. With il Borghetto in San Gennaro relatively under control, it was time to come up with Plan B for Project Arsina, la Porcellaia.

We have a charming neighbor across the valley from us at la Casa Gialla. The acoustics are such that we can yell across the valley and hear each other, even though it must be a quarter mile away in a direct line. He is a well-known architect and he and his geologist wife have become friends of ours. His name is Massimo Rocco. I love that name. If I come back in another life, I want to be named Massimo Rocco. *Massimo* means maximum - you can't get better than that. And even though *Rocco* doesn't translate into anything in English, it has that macho, rock-hard sound that I love.

More than friends, Massimo and I are occasional golf opponents when we have an *Italiani v Stranieri* golf match. It's the Italians, Vittorio, my *commercialista*, and Massimo, against my best mate, Jeff, from Australia, and me. It's a spirited competition with lots of insults, taught to them by us, I'm afraid. Trash talk is not usually their style.

Massimo was well aware of our problems with la Porcellaia. There was no market for five expensive apartments in two buildings, which is what we got permission to build years earlier. Your building permit expires with the *Comune* after five years and that is what we faced now. We didn't have the will or the money to start it after the housing market crashed in 2008, so we let the permit expire.

Massimo came to the rescue. He called us in for a meeting and he pitched the idea that we would have much better luck using our 8,600 square feet of former pig sty to build three luxury homes of almost 3,000 square feet each, with private gardens and swimming pools. Knowing we had spent over €100,000 for designs, *geometras* and the permission process for il Borghetto, I told him I loved the idea but we couldn't afford to pay him at the front end of the process. He graciously offered to do all the designs and renderings, take it through the *permesso* process with the *Comune* and the *Belle Arte*, and I could pay him after we had sold one or more of the homes.

Another savior had entered my life. It was not only a kind gesture by Massimo, but it said to me that he felt this new plan would attract buyers; otherwise, he wouldn't be taking the risk. He doesn't get paid if we don't find a buyer. I needed that boost in confidence before risking any more money on la Porcellaia. I'm thrilled that we have a new plan.

I often think about how much my life has changed in the years we have lived in Lucca. I had a wonderful business career full of exciting opportunities to travel the world. For the final four years of my business life, I was the head of a small company and Debbie and I were in London, the city we loved.

Now on most every Saturday in the summer, I find myself making beds, preparing welcome baskets, fluffing and buffing, and getting ready to greet another European family as they arrive for their dream vacation at il Borghetto. And I love it. We have had the most wonderful guests and as I see the look of delight on the children's faces when I walk the family up to the pool as part of their welcome tour, it gives me a renewed sense of pride in what we have accomplished.

Anderò has well and truly been a financial disaster. But there is no doubt that il Borghetto is an artistic success.

I often think back to the times when Nicola and his team reached an important point in the construction process and I would be on hand to either make a key decision or to just admire their skills. One of the most significant moments was when it was time to lay the handmade terracotta tiles in each apartment. Handmade tiles means that no two tiles are the same. They each have little bumps, ridges, and color variations that give them character unlike machine-made tiles.

The tubes that would carry the hot water for our in-floor heating were all in place, snaking through every foot of the floor. Now it was time to decide which pattern to choose for the laying of the tiles. I thought this would be an easy decision. The tiles are 15cm x 30cm (about 6 inches by 12 inches), perfect rectangles. The pattern I had firmly in my mind was to have a couple of rows of tiles squared-up to the walls as a border, with the traditional herringbone pattern laid out in a 45-degree angle for the interior of the floor.

I arrived one morning to see that they had laid out about 20% of the first living room floor and were waiting for my approval. I was a bit surprised to see the tiles laid out completely squared-up with the walls, with each row alternating lengthwise and widthwise across the floor. It didn't look very imaginative to me. Then Nicola pulled me aside to explain, "This pattern goes back hundreds of years. If you look at some the important villas and major buildings from the 1600s and 1700s, this is the pattern you will see." He told me about a couple of historic buildings in Centro Storico to go visit and see for myself. I did and I immediately saw the beauty in this simple pattern. We did it his way. The floors are stunning.

This was one of the first times in a long series of instances where Nicola and his team would look at something and make a recommendation or a decision that would turn out to be perfect . Their *buon occhio* was right time and time again. With no formal training as artists or architects, they instinctively know how to finish off a stair-step with a perfect little lip; how to calculate the dimensions of a custom-made table top to look aesthetically pleasing; and how to lay a handmade terracotta floor. Now I smile inside whenever I look down upon this beautiful pattern in each apartment at il Borghetto.

On arrival day for our new guests, I am particularly pleased to hear them say "wow" when they walk into their apartment. Our apartments are unique and inviting and are especially beautiful and welcoming when guests arrive after dark. Many of them drive down from Northern Europe. They have been in the car for eight hours, sometimes for two days in a row. They are tired, thirsty and hungry. I break out a bottle of Prosecco and we have a toast to their upcoming holiday.

The first thing I show them is a photo of il

Borghetto as we found it in 2007, the photo that you see on the cover of the book. A massive building of old bricks and stone, falling down in places, with traces of every window and every door that we copied in the new building, this photo shares some of the rich history of il Borghetto with our guests. Their smiles and excitement at being here warm my heart.

I know now that it wasn't just for financial reasons that made me want to finish il Borghetto. Families have lived on this spot for over 500 years. This building deserved to be brought back to life; to bring joy to hundreds of families in the coming years. I remember walking through the newly finished apartments in 2014 on my own. I remember asking myself who would live within these walls in the years to come? Who would have the vacation of their life here? Who would make this apartment their own, bringing their children and grandchildren here in the coming years, to splash in the pool in this peaceful setting looking up at the village of San Gennaro?

I remember saying to myself, "Bless all those who enter here. May il Borghetto in San Gennaro bring them all great joy."

Chapter 13 -- The Olive Harvest

The ten-year (and counting) saga that is Anderò has not consume me emotionally every day. There were times of the year when I could put my problems aside, the happiest of those times being when my cousins flew in from the US for the annual tradition that has become the highlight of our thirteen years in Lucca. The olive harvest (*la raccolta*) symbolizes so much of what is wonderful about Italians and life in Italy:

- A respect for nature, food, and the Italians' penchant for wasting nothing.
- The importance of family above all; represented by the sharing of the oil that takes place after the harvest.
- A focus on health, with everyone recognizing the importance of having pure, extra virgin olive oil as part of his or her daily life.

After our neighbors made us the offer we couldn't refuse and sold us some land surrounding our Casa Gialla, we were now the proud owners of 35 olive trees. We were excited as November 2006 approached and we were about to do our first olive harvest. I rushed out and bought the necessary equipment:

Nets

Gloves

Pins to join the nets together once they are laid

Hand rakes for picking by hand

Crates

Bamboo poles

And most importantly: an electric
picker and a car battery to run it

Before we picked our first olive I was side-
tracked by something more important; just as I
was side-tracked about what we were going to
name our new company before I came up with
the name Anderò. We needed a label for our
oil, even if we weren't going to be selling it.

At the end of our first year at la Casa Gialla,
our neighbor's cat had a litter of three male
kittens. "Do you want one?" he asked.
"Because if you don't, I'm just going to drown
them." He wasn't kidding. Italians have a
somewhat unusual relationship with their pets.
Cats are almost always outdoor cats and little
spaying is done to keep the population under
control. In many cases, they also keep their
dogs outside, sometimes in a kennel. When a
farmer's hunting dog becomes too old or too
scared to hunt, he is frequently abandoned.

Our neighbor already had two cats and he wanted to keep only one of the new litter. "Why don't you take two?" he said. "They will keep each other company." And that is how the adorable Macchia and Pino came into our lives. We originally named one of them Josepina after our good friend, Jo, in Kentucky, as she was a great cat lover. Then one day we discovered that our Josepina was a Josepino so we had to make a small adjustment. He became Pino. His brother has a small white spot on the back of his neck, about the only way to tell them apart. So we named him Macchia. For all you coffee-loving, non-Italian speakers, a *caffè macchiato* is an espresso with a spot of milk in it, as opposed to the more generous dose of foamy milk in a *cappuccino*. So we have a cat named Spot, Italian style.

It then became an obvious decision to name our olive oil *Due Gattini*, Two Kittens, because they were six months old just before our first harvest. We took an sweet photo of them nuzzling each other for the label. There we had it, our first year's label:

Due Gattini

Jim and Debbie's

Lucca   Extra Virgin   2006

Organic Olive Oil

It is still our label to this day, even though the
due gattini are no longer kittens but now are
due gatti, and one is on the plump side. They
love to be on the hillside with us when we do
the olive harvest. They run under the nets and
create havoc.

Friends of ours who had been picking olives
from about 300 trees for many years shared
their secrets with us on how to do the harvest.
Prune the trees lightly each year to keep the
middle open to encourage air circulation,
preventing mold and fungus from growing on
the leaves. Cut back all suckers – new growth
that goes straight up and doesn't bear any

fruit. Fertilize the trees in the spring, just before a rain, so it can soak in. Keep the grass cut short during the spring and just before the harvest to discourage fruit flies. Some of the local farmers spray each year when it looks like the fruit flies are about to invade. We never do. I'd rather have a little protein in my olive oil than to spray. Besides, all impurities settle to the bottom of the 30-liter stainless steel storage can after a few weeks.

The farmers tell me they are spraying with something that is *bio,* the Italian word for organic. The product is called *Rame,* which is a copper-based spray and needs to be well controlled and applied repeatedly in the summer. Even though it is not supposed to penetrate the fruit itself, the fact that you cannot use it by law within sixty days of *la raccolta* is enough evidence for me to say no thanks. As I tell my friends, yes copper is *bio.* And by definition, all of the elements are *bio.* Therefore, arsenic is *bio.* We don't spray.

The olive harvest itself is an amazing experience. I can make it sound like the most romantic, most satisfying thing a non-farmer can do. But it's hard work. I feel a bit like Tom Sawyer, selling our friends and family on what a romantic adventure I could let them in on, to come over and paint this picket fence....um; I mean pick these olives. I can fool all of them once. Only the hardy ones and the ones who want to be paid in *Due Gattini* come back a second and third time.

That would be my cousins. I have two wonderful cousins, Cherryl and Pam, who are sisters living in the States. They and their husbands, Tom and Jules, love to come over for the olive harvest because they know they will be going home with many liters of the liquid gold that will get them through an entire year until the next harvest.

The taste of our oil is sublime, like nothing you have ever tasted from a bottle of store-bought olive oil. Each year the characteristics vary for many reasons; the primary two being the weather during the growing season and the time of year when we pick the olives. Unlike grapes, which are tracked by the day and then by the hour for the perfect time to harvest, when the sugar and tannins are at their perfect moments, olives can be harvested over a longer period of time. From late October through the end of December, the olive mill cooperatives are open to receive their customers, ready to turn your hundreds of kilos of olives into delicious oil.

We have often been asked by novices, "Do you grow green olives or black olives?" Seems like a reasonable question. But while there are dozens of varietals of olive trees, each yielding a slightly larger or smaller olive, and with leaves that vary in size and color, all olives start out green and then blacken as they ripen. While most fruits turn sweeter as they ripen, olives do not. If you pick an olive from the tree and taste it, regardless of the color, you will be greatly disappointed. They taste awful. Bitter. It makes you wonder who discovered what a wonderful fruit this could be, and that its oil would eventually be in ultra-high demand in almost every country in the world. The table olives we eat have been soaked, rinsed, and seasoned with salt, spices and herbs to eventually give us something delicious to pop into our mouth – or into a martini. It takes weeks, and sometimes months, depending on the recipe, to turn an olive into something edible.

Not so with the oil. It is ready to be tasted and enjoyed the minute you come home from the *frantoio* (mill).

By the third or fourth year of the harvest, we started to feel like seasoned farmers and now after twelve years, we confidently attack the hill and we have our timing down. But in the first couple of years it was a bit of a farce out there. Here is rule number one: Don't sign up a picking crew where more than one of the members has OCD. Since this seems to run in my family, and I can't say no to any of them, we have quite a scene at 9:00 a.m. on the first day.

We go into our *magazzino* and drag out all the nets, picks, poles, picker, battery, crates…..no, wait. That is what we <u>should</u> be doing. But we're not. Before they flew over from the States, we told them to just pack their hiking boots so they could manage the steep hillside, and we would furnish them with all the warm-weather gear they might need. So before any work gets done they are pawing through our plastic storage bins trying on sweatshirts, caps, jackets and bandanas. They know photos will be taken during the day, so they want to look their best.

It's 10:00 a.m. now and we have yet to start.

Our land is difficult to work. On half of it we have about one dozen trees on a hill that is so steep that they built terraces into the hillside to make it easier to climb up and down. Easier, not easy. The terrace steps are just high enough that you can't go up or down them in a single step. You usually end up sliding on your butt if you're going downhill; and clawing your way up the face of the terrace if you're going uphill. The other half of our land with the rest of the trees is slightly less steep, with no terraces -- easier to work.

Unfortunately our trees are not all laid out in nice straight rows. I imagine when our neighbors sold us this land they were quietly celebrating that they were getting rid of a piece of land that was their most difficult to harvest. On the hill above our home, which is not our property, the trees are lined up in nice straight rows, making it much easier to put nets under a dozen or more trees at a time.

That is the first step. You spend quite a bit of time laying out the nets and pinning them together under the trees. Then you pick the olives on those trees, roll them downhill in the nets, crate them, and then net another group of trees. The fewer times you have to pick up and move the nets the better. Our trees zig and zag such that in some places we can only net three of them at a time. Very inefficient. Those friends I mentioned who harvest 300 trees each year can pick fifty trees a day with just the two of them. My inexperienced crew and I will take three days to pick 35 trees.

Starting at 10:00 a.m. is only part of the problem.

Once we are dressed and looking good we find ourselves standing at the very top of our property looking straight down at 40 meters of steeply pitched terraces. Then the fun begins. The nets are about 4 meters wide and 25 meters long. We have a dozen of them.

"I think we should lay the nets across the hill this year," says OCD cousin No. 1.

"No, we laid them across the hill last year and I didn't like that. I think we should lay them going up and down the hill," pipes in OCD cousin No. 2. Debbie chimes in as well but I'm not going there. I make the final decision and note the first signs of grumbling from the picking crew.

Once you get the first net positioned and stretched out, you lay another net next to it. Then you have to do the most difficult job – joining the nets together with plastic pins so there are no holes or gaps through which the olives can escape when you knock them down.

You are on your hands and knees, putting a pin through both nets every meter or two.

This is an art. When I drive down our hill I see beautifully netted olive groves that look like the nets are welded together. Not a gap anywhere. Our nets meander around a bit and as soon as some well-intentioned person with OCD thinks, "Oh, I'll just pick up the edge of this net and give it a tug to straighten it out" the whole section below it opens up gaps, that then have to be re-tugged and re-joined. We were hopeless.

It's 11:30 now. We have not yet picked a single olive. I'm starting to feel stressed.

My family doesn't work well without alcohol. So once the dust has settled as to which way we are going to lay the nets and I have four of them on their hands and knees pinning away, I go off to the house to make hot chocolate for them. With a splash of grappa in it. Just to keep them going. "A happy picker is a productive picker," that's my motto.

We pick for about one hour and then I am back

in the house again, preparing lunch for my hungry crew. I am dissed repeatedly by my family for disappearing. They accuse me of running off to check my e-mail every hour. I accuse them of slacking off as they stand around watching the person with the electric picker knock down the olives.

It's lunchtime. We all gather under the pergola by the pool and I bring out a steaming pot of minestrone, followed by *spaghetti con aglio, pepperoncino, prezzemolo e olio di olive Due Gattini*. The red wine flows. We laugh and catch up on our lives in the year it has been since we've seen each other.

After lunch there are only three hours of daylight left. We pick some more, roll the olives downhill, crate them, and do some netting so that we can get off to an earlier start the next morning. I'm dismayed to see only four crates of olives in the *magazzino* from our day's efforts. We need about twenty crates before we can go to the *frantoio*. You have to reserve your time slot days in advance, as they are booked solid from early morning through midnight during the peak harvest season. Our appointment is at 4:00 p.m. in two days time. I try not to panic as we crack open the *Prosecco* and start cooking our evening meal. More wine flows.

The next day we start to get in a rhythm, even though a couple of the crew have wandered out of the house to start picking at 9:30 a.m., having been distracted by my electric whizzer that froths the hot milk for their morning *cappuccino*.

Before the electric olive picker came along, the harvest was all done by hand. Running your hands down a branch with just enough pressure to pop off the olives, while leaving the leaves behind, is a sensual pleasure. You still see farmers picking totally by hand – some working the lower branches this way while others use bamboo poles to whack the branches above to get them to give up their olives. It is slow. It is peaceful. No one is in a hurry. You hit a few branches and knock down some olives. When you can't see any more olives in the part of the tree where you are working, you take one or two steps to the side and a whole new vista of olives opens up to you. It is like you and the olives are playing this quiet game of hide-and-seek. It takes patience to find them all amongst the leaves and branches.

This hand-picking method is why olive trees are pruned to stay short. Over many years as you cut away the growth in the middle and any new branches that grow straight up, your trees start to look like umbrellas. Branches grow gracefully upward, then curve outward and bend back down toward the ground. That's where you will find most of the olives. Yes, you can climb up into the middle of the tree and use a ladder to reach the higher branches, but that is dangerous. Better to work with shorter trees. The local hospitals get frequent visits during harvest season from farmers who have fallen out of a tree chasing just one more olive.

The electric picker came along and now we can reach the higher limbs, which allows us to let the trees grow a bit taller. The picker is a long aluminum pole that telescopes out to about four meters in length. There is a small motor at the top of the pole and then a plate with six long carbon fiber fingers attached. When you turn it on, connected to a car battery sitting on the ground or hooked up to a tractor engine, the carbon fiber fingers gyrate in an asymmetrical pattern at high speed.

You gently place these pulsating sticks against the branches of the tree to rattle them, and the olives go flying in all directions. It is really a thrill when you get the picker positioned amongst a particularly thick bunch of olives and you see (and feel) dozens of them flying at once. If you are standing directly under the tree you are pelted with olives; hitting you in the head, going down your shirt, and making you giggle all at the same time. We wear protective goggles, as getting hit in the eye with an olive flying down from the sky is dangerous.

There are variations on the electric picker. The most popular is the same pole, but at the head there are what appear to be two rakes that slap back and forth against each other at high speed. The idea is to knock down the olives while not disturbing the leaves. Almost all of the excess leaves and debris that end up in your crates have to be removed before you go to the *frantoio*.

The most efficient way to do the harvest is to have the electric picker running every minute. You get tired holding this up over your head, so we trade off every half hour or so. But the idea is to keep netting ahead of the picker so that when you are done harvesting one section, the picker can move on to the next set of trees while the other members of the crew roll the nets and olives downhill to crate them up.

The picker makes a bit of noise but it is efficient. However, you have to be careful not to push the carbon fiber fingers against any thick branches or else they could break or the motor could seize up. This happened to us one year and I had to rush off to the *agraria* where I bought it to see if they could fix it. The ball bearings inside the motor needed to be re-packed. "Come back in 24 hours" he told me.

So for a full day we had to pick by hand. Debbie and cousin Cherryl (OCD No. 1) hand-picked the lower part of one of our biggest trees, and Tom and I climbed up into the tree and worked the upper branches. It was quiet and peaceful. We could talk quietly to each other without having to shout over the whir of the electric picker. Cherryl said it was her favorite day of picking ever.

By the end of day two we have seven more crates full of olives in the *magazzino*. I do a quick calculation and realize we won't have enough olives unless we bring in some help on day three.

An emergency call is placed to Doug.

Younger, stronger Doug.

Able to hold the electric picker for hours at a time without taking a break, Doug.

He saves our harvest.

Faced with a 4:00 p.m. appointment, day three is just a blur. Not only do we need to knock down and gather about nine more crates of olives, we have to carry the crates, each one weighing 45 – 50 pounds, from the *magazzino* up to the car. Did I mention we live on a hill? This is back-breaking work and once we have the crates up near the car we have to go through them and remove as many leaves and sticks as possible. We have to be at the *frantoio* 30 minutes before our appointment, to unload the car and take our place in the queue.

We start to load up two cars for the trip to the *frantoio*. But wait! Before we can do that, more photos have to be taken of the picking crew standing around, admiring our 20 crates of olives in front of the cars. This is just about the point where we can see the light at the end of the tunnel as we high-five each other over the quantity of olives we have gathered over the past three days. We each dig our hands down into the middle of a crate, gently turning the olives over, removing the last few twigs and leaves. There is a lot of blood, sweat and tears in those twenty crates. All disagreements about which way the nets should run have been forgotten (and we will forget to take notes as to how we did it; thus, we have the same argument every year). The anticipation of tasting our new oil a few hours from now gives us new energy.

The Frantoio

The *frantoio* is an amazing place. A large factory building with millions of euros worth of shiny equipment inside, and all of it used for only about eight weeks a year. There are only a few modern mills in our area, plus dozens of the old-fashioned, cold-press mills still in use. Thousands of farmers come to these mills every autumn to turn their olives into oil.

The spicy smell of olive oil overwhelms you when you walk in the door. The equipment runs continuously for 18 or more hours a day. If we get a few days of rain it throws the schedule into chaos. It is too dangerous to pick on a hillside in the rain, so appointments get cancelled and need to be rescheduled for when it is dry again. But the mill is already booked solid for weeks in advance, so the only way the *frantoio* can accommodate its customers is to extend their working hours far into the night. It happened to us one rainy autumn, when the only time slot available after we had to cancel our original appointment, was either 5:30 a.m. or midnight. We chose midnight.

We were invited to a friend's house for dinner that night, so in the afternoon we loaded up the car with our olives, showered and got dressed for the dinner party. We said goodbye to our hosts at 11:00 p.m. and drove off to the mill. Debbie felt a bit self-conscious about being the only wife there in Prada boots, unloading olives from the car.

They have a wonderful system at the mill to ensure that you get back the oil from your own olives, while at the same time processing the crop from five other farmers. This means the *frantoio* is teeming with your fellow farmers as you arrive. There is only one drop-off point to unload your olives and here is where the fun begins. I pull my car into the crowded courtyard and immediately feel conspicuous because I am surrounded by proper farm vehicles. The most popular are the little *Apes* (bees), which are tiny farm trucks with a truck bed in the back and thin, cantilevered tires to handle the weight. It is also obvious that I am a *straniero*, a foreigner. Several other farmers are standing next to their fully laden vehicles, staring at the doorway where someone is unloading their olives.

"Buonasera! Chi è l'ultimo?" I ask one of the farmers. Who is the last one in the queue? As I ask the question I size up the competition to see how long I will have to wait. This is the most delicate part of the trek to the *frantoio*. I must project *bella figura*, while at the same time not let anyone take my rightful place in line. Italians dislike waiting in line and in my early years here I cringed every time I walked into the *paneficio* or the *macelleria* (the bakery and the butcher) to find a half-dozen people standing around in no particular pattern or order. Pharmacies, banks, and the post office have now instituted a take-a-number system to prevent any disputes, but in other shops, people just come in, sit down, and go to the

counter when they know it is their turn. I have since learned that this system works even when there is no take-a-number system. You just find out who is *l'ultimo* and you follow him.

You are supposed to arrive at the *frantoio* thirty minutes before your appointment. If everyone followed this rule there would not be a long wait because they can only process about four customers an hour. But of course the Italians don't always follow the rules. I once read that Italy produces more laws than any other EU country; then they take great pride in ignoring as many of them as they can.

If I am just one or two farmers from the front of the queue to unload my olives, I wait my turn. But if the crowd is bigger I have to start asking questions. This is where I am happy when Debbie is by my side. Debbie can charm anyone and I don't mean in a manipulative way. She genuinely loves talking to people and she has the nicest demeanor as she chats up the farmers, trying to sort out why there are so many of us there at the same time. But most years I am dropping off the olives on my own as the car is packed to the roof with olives, with no room for a passenger.

So the interrogation begins. *"Mi scusi, ma quando è il suo appuntamento?"* I ask one of less grumpy looking ones. It turns out his appointment is many hours from now, and he is dropping his olives off early because he is probably bringing another load at his appointed time. I politely explain to him that my appointment is in 30 minutes and the mill has asked me to come 30 minutes *in anticipo* (in advance). A grunt…. a sigh….and a reluctant *"Dai,"* (go ahead) usually follows. A couple of other conversations like this and I have moved up in the queue, usually with no bad feelings.

I have only had to go inside once to speak with the supervisor to explain that I'm here on time for my appointment but I can't get to the unloading dock because of the queue. He walks outside with his clipboard and starts asking questions. Voices are raised. Arms are waved in the air. Shoulders are shrugged. The man with the clipboard turns to me and says,

"Avanti." Come forward. As I back my car into the loading dock, I try not to make eye contact with the four farmers I have just ticked off.

Now the fun begins. I unload our twenty crates into two large bins. The man with the clipboard comes along with a forklift and takes our haul over to his industrial scale where they are weighed. *Due quintali* is the minimum you can bring to the mill. 200 kilos (440 pounds). In the ten years we have been coming to the mill, we average between 325 and 375 kilos of olives. And while they weigh your olives at the beginning of the process, it is the weight of the oil that you take home at the end of the process that is important. Your yield, the percentage of wet weight to dry weight, is a number that is shared, bragged about, bemoaned and logged into all our notes for future reference. For that is what this is all about.

"How much oil did you walk away with?" other farmers will ask you.

"14.5%" I tell them. "Bravo! Buono!" is the response.

They don't care how many liters you have produced. That's not important. Your yield is what is important. I didn't understand the significance of this the first few years we did the harvest. When my neighbor would ask me what my yield was, I proudly told him that we came home with 50 liters of oil from the 20 crates that we took to the mill. He looked at me and asked me again. I explained again. I thought, "Dammit, my Italian isn't that bad!" But he only cared about the yield percentage, not the number of liters.

The significance of the yield has hit home to me as the years have gone by. Your yield is different every year and depends on many things. How ripe are your olives? How much rain have you had? Did you pick early or late in the season? Each of these factors impacts the yield and determines how much oil you walk away with.

How ripe? The weather determines how fast

your olives ripen and turn black. An extra hot spring will set things in motion faster and the olives will ripen earlier in the autumn.

How much rain? The more rain, the more water (and weight) in your olives. This will lower your yield. That is because the water is spun out of the olives during processing. You pay by the weight of the olives you bring to the mill, so some of the old-timers don't harvest until December, when the olives have started to shrivel and have a lower percentage of water in them.

When do you harvest? The mills start to open at the end of October. The next six to eight weeks is the prime harvesting season. The earlier you pick, generally the lower the yield. On average, when we take our olives to the mill, they are about 25% black and 75% green. The higher percentage of green olives in your mix, the spicier and more peppery your oil will be, which is what we like. We tend to harvest early, in the first two weeks of November, primarily to tie into our Thanksgiving celebrations.

The yield percentage can vary from about 10% all the way up to 18% or higher, under the right circumstances. It can make a big difference. If you go to the mill with *tre quintale*, 300 kilos of olives, and you get a 10% yield, your 30 kilos of olive oil equates to 33 liters of oil.

But if you are lucky, your yield percentage could be 18%, which would turn that same batch of 300 kilos of olives into 59 liters of oil. I never realized how important each percentage point of yield was until I observed what happens at the end of the process at the *frantoio*.

It's a lovely ritual to watch as one family after another take their position at the end of the production line, where a single spigot is waiting to deliver their oil. There are often two or three generations in attendance. Cousins, uncles, grandfathers. This is their olive oil for the entire year. As the oil comes out to fill their stainless steel can of 20, 30, or 50 liters, they put the lid on the can and drag it over to the industrial scale to weigh it. Two or three of them have calculators.

When all their oil is on the scale, the distribution begins. No doubt they have decided long before that cousin Luigi's share is 12% of the total. *Nonno* and *nonna* may get 25%. Other assorted members take their share based on how many trees each of them has, who has done the work, who is doing the cooking for the next twelve months; or based on the that's-how-it-has -been-done-in-their-family-for-100-years method.

No one tries to pour the oil from the large containers into one or two-liter bottles at the mill. You can do that at home. For larger amounts, the distribution is done immediately. Cousin Luigi's 12%, for example, might be 15 kilos of oil by weight, which translates to 16.5 liters. Funnels at the ready, they pour 15 kilos of oil into a large plastic container for him, having carefully allowed for the weight of the container, and he goes home a happy man.

This ritual goes on for family after family. It always makes me smile. It shows how much the Italians revere and respect this basic commodity of life. Olive oil represents health. It represents life. They have spent hours and hours in their olive groves during the year pruning, weed-whacking, fertilizing and harvesting. This oil has to last them for the entire year.

They know the tricks that go into the bottles of olive oil that are sold at the supermarket at low prices. Olive oil that is "packed in Italy" doesn't mean the olives came from Italy. The demand for Italian olive oil worldwide far outstrips the supply. So olives are brought to southern Italy from all over the Mediterranean, to be combined with Italian olive oil and sold off by the big producers to an unsuspecting world as Italian Extra Virgin oil. Italy long ago brought strict controls to their wine industry, which was similarly devious in the 1960s and 1970s. Now you can rely on the DOC labeling of the finer wines in Italy, and respect for Italian wine has dramatically increased as a result. These controls don't yet exist in the world of olive oil production and distribution.

That's why most of our friends and neighbors are proud of the fact that they have never purchased olive oil from the store in their life.

Back at the mill, we wait our turn to have our olives processed. When the time comes, the forklift driver takes our giant bins of olives and dumps them into the receiving hopper. From there they are transported up a conveyor belt where air-jets blow away the leaves and sticks that we have invariably missed. The olives get washed, crushed (pits and all) and your mash gets piped into one of six holding tanks. Your name is displayed above your holding tank and you eagerly peek through the cloudy window to see the color of your mash. It resembles thick porridge at this point. The color ranges from light, greenish brown to dark brown and there is frequently a hint of red in the mix. Giant blades gently turn the mash and the holding tank heats the mixture to kill any bacteria.

When your mash arrives in your holding tank there are five tanks ahead of you in the process. You have about a one-hour wait for the next step, as the holding tanks in front of you are processed. The excitement begins to build. You watch the family in front of you take their turn at the spigot with their shiny clean stainless steel cans. And as the last drops from their batch dribble into their can, they put the lid on and move over to the scales.

The master controller nods at me. It's our turn. The cousins are getting excited. I'm excited.

He clicks a few icons on his computer screen and our mash is pumped out of our holding tank into a centrifuge. The mash is spun at high speed and behind the scenes, the water is separated and goes down the drain. The pit, which has been crushed and now looks like fine black sand, is spun off and piped outside the mill into giant holding tanks. This will be trucked away and spun again to get more oil; then the residue will be fed to the pigs. The Italians waste nothing.

We are standing at the spigot. Our 30-liter cans are in position. Then, with an opening glug, the first of our oil spurts out. This moment is always emotional for me, for several reasons. The oil is green, shiny and almost iridescent some years. It's a slightly different color from year to year. It is cloudy at this point but after weeks in the stainless steel container, it becomes a bit more clear, while still retaining its sharp green color.

But that isn't why it's an emotional moment for me. It's what the oil represents. Our muscles ache from climbing up and down the hills. We are tired. I think about the suckers that I have trimmed from the tree during the year so that more energy can go to the olives. I think about all the times I went out to inspect the olives, hoping that the fruit flies have chosen to pass us by. I worry months in advance that the week we have chosen to harvest due to the cousins' flight schedule, might be a total washout due to rain.

Mostly, I think about the joy of tasting our new oil, which we will resist until we get home.

One 30-liter can is filled. We place the second one under the spigot. We run over to the holding tank to peek inside, trying to estimate how much more oil will arrive. Will our second can be big enough? Most years we get from 45 to 55 liters of oil from our trees, so we have only invested in the two 30-liter stainless steel containers. We can always buy more containers from the mill, but just as our second can reaches 80 or 90% capacity, the oil flow slows and we know the end is near. Another minute and the flow becomes a dribble. The master controller nods at me again and presses some buttons to shift from our holding tank to the next.

We put the lid on our second can and drag it onto the scale. We have weighed our empty stainless steel cans. 2.5 kilos each. We add the weight of our two full containers together, subtract the weight of the cans, and divide that by the dry weight of the olives we brought to the mill. It is the moment of reckoning. 15.2% Yes! An excellent yield. We're thrilled. We stop into the office to report our numbers and pay. The bill comes out to only about one euro per liter. I don't know how they do that. We happily pay and head for home.

The most memorable harvest we ever had was in 2012. The moon and stars seemed to align that year. No fruit flies, combined with quite a bit of rain leading up to the harvest, meant that the olives were plump and heavy. We had an abundance of pickers with Tom and Cherryl coming over from the States, combined with a friend from London and three more Lucchese friends. We had 22 crates of olives after just two days, with one day remaining before our appointment at the *frantoio*. So Tom, Cherryl and I took the picker and went over to la Porcellaia, where we own 100 trees that have not been pruned for many years. It doesn't matter. Olives have grown on unpruned olive trees for thousands of years and they are plentiful this year at Arsina.

The hillside there is far steeper than ours at home so we chose a half dozen of the easiest trees to pick and went to work. Eight more crates! It took two trips to get our 30 crates to the *frantoio* and we all tried to guess how many kilos we had picked. When they placed our bins on the scale and it registered 564 kilos (1,240 pounds) we were blown away. We knew it would be a couple of hours before our turn at the spigot would arrive, so we snuck off to a local bar and shared a bottle of *Prosecco* to celebrate our record harvest.

But how much oil would we get? We all sat around the table with a calculator trying to estimate how many liters would come pouring out. We had brought four extra 3-liter bottles with us, so combined with our two 30-liter stainless steel containers, we were ready for 72 liters. Our previous best result had been 54 liters.

The magic moment arrived. Eight of us have come to the mill. There are 20 or so other people there, waiting their turn. Our oil comes gushing out. We start to get excited as we fill our second 30-liter can and there is still some of our mash left in our holding tank. We carefully fill our 3-liter bottles one at a time. The oil keeps coming.

There is a small shut-off valve you can use to

stop the flow while you are switching containers and your oil then builds up in a small reservoir while you do this. You don't have much time. We need more containers. In a panic, we send Cherryl, who knows fewer words of Italian than any of the rest of us, scampering into the office to try to explain that we need to buy some empty 3-liter tin cans *subito*! (right away).

There can't be much more oil but I shout, "Buy 3 of them!" as she runs off, "just in case."

She comes back just in time for us to release what's in the reservoir and we quickly fill the 3 new tins, 9 liters worth. And the oil is still coming.

"Go buy 3 more!" I yell at Cherryl. Off she goes.

By this time, the 20 or so others have gathered around to watch this circus of inept *stranieri* at the spigot. "Why the hell didn't they just buy another 30-liter can?" is what I imagine they must be saying to each other.

Cherryl is back with three more tins and we release the pent-up oil again. Just when I think that we're going to need to go back to the office for a third time, the flow of oil starts to slow down, dribbles, and stops just as our 10th and final 3-liter tin can is full.

It's incredible. We've produced 90 liters of olive oil!

I want to quickly get all our oil onto the scales, record the weight, and get out of the mill as fast as possible. "How embarrassing," I thought. "They are going to be talking about us for weeks." After the weighing, everyone takes a couple of the 3-liter tins and I grab the hand trolley provided for customers to wheel the 30 and 50-liter cans out to your car. I slide one of our 30-liter cans onto the trolley, tilt it back on its wheels, and head for the door.

"*Attenzione!*" cry out some of the Italians as we are ten feet from the door. I look down and oil is dribbling out of the top of the can where we had not fully tightened the lid. We've left a thin line of oil ten feet long across the floor.

Beautiful, fresh, new oil. Now we have committed the ultimate sin in an Italian's eyes. We're wasting olive oil. We grab some paper towels, clean up our mess, and slink out of the mill.

Did I say that they were going to talk about us for weeks? Make that years.

Even today, I kid Cherryl that she is not allowed back in the *frantoio* because she has been banned. We should all be banned. The next year I jokingly suggested we should all wear a disguise when we go back.

The Dinner

The reason we book our appointment at the mill for 4:00 p.m. every year is simple. It takes between two and three hours from the time you arrive until the time you leave with your oil. And we have planned a feast.

We have already stocked up on fresh *focaccia* and everything else we need for dinner. The rule is, every dish must showcase the new oil. *Cannellini* bean salad with diced red pepper, fennel and red onion. A green salad. A simple pasta with the new Due Gattini as the star ingredient. Because we usually have some oil left over from the previous year, we pour some of that into bowls so we can compare. Most years, we get together with five or six friends after the last one has done their harvest, and we all proudly display our oil and we have a tasting. The colors and levels of spiciness vary but they are all delicious.

We take photos. You would have thought we had just delivered a baby. All of us look lovingly at the little tasting bowls of our new oil on the table. And then we break off a piece of *focaccia*, dunk it in the new oil, and taste.

If you have never tasted new oil, still warm from the *frantoio*, it is like nothing you have ever experienced before. While store-bought oil is often bland and tasteless, new oil is just the opposite. It is spicy. You let it linger on the back of your tongue and you can feel the burn. It is peppery. It is heaven. Last year's oil has mellowed, as they all do, into a softer feel on your palate. It is still delicious but not

as peppery as the new oil. Light and air are the
enemies of olive oil and that is why we keep
our oil in the light-tight, air-tight stainless steel
containers throughout the year, only drawing
off what we need a half-liter at a time.

Dinner is *squisito*. We all sink into our chairs,
crack open another bottle of Chianti Classico
Riserva, and settle in for the evening.
Knowing we don't have to go back out onto
the hillside tomorrow makes us giddy. Our
bodies ache but we don't care. The fact that
our nets are still out there, strewn across the
hills, doesn't faze us. We can gather those and
neatly roll them and tie them up another day.
Tonight, it's all about tasting the oil.

Chapter 14 -- From Toledo to Tuscany

Growing up in Toledo, Ohio, I could never have imagined the life I have lived. My brother, Mike, and I had two loving parents who didn't say, "I love you," often enough, but who showed us their love every day. Mike and I were supported in whatever path we took in life. Our Mom's only guidance was, "Do what makes you happy."

Two years older than me, Mike was my role model. Always the better baseball and basketball player, and student, he was a quiet inspiration for me all through high school. His life path was to raise a family early while mine took me to university, but our parents were always there for both of us, financially and emotionally. They worked full time and our Dad took on an extra job at night as treasurer of his local credit union in order to make ends meet.

When I left Toledo for good at age eighteen, my vision went no further than planning how I was going to get through the next semester of school. I could never have predicted my future homes after graduating from Ohio University.

Sioux City, Iowa
San Francisco
Rochester, NY
Mission Viejo, CA
San Francisco
London
Washington, DC
Chicago
Stockholm
London
Lucca

My life's path has also taken me on some creative adventures through the culinary world. Coming from a home where meatloaf and canned green beans featured regularly, I became interested in cooking in San Francisco in my thirties, when I discovered that it was a good way to impress women. Then in London, Debbie sent me off to a six-week cooking course at Leiths School of Food and Wine. I soon figured out that Debbie wasn't doing this only for my benefit. Later, as my career evolved into bigger and more stressful jobs, I found that cooking dinner after a tough day was a great stress reducer for me, and my interest in fine food and great cooking continued to grow. I was helped along by my wonderful European Kodak friends who took me to Michelin starred restaurants in France; the best underground caves of Gamla Stan in Stockholm, where salmon was served every way imaginable; and to Milan and Florence, hosted by my good friend, Enrico, another foodophile. The full week of cooking classes near Arezzo before Doris and Doug's wedding pushed me to the next level.

Our *forno* has brought us much joy as we have

hosted many poolside dinners under the wisteria-covered pergola. Hundreds of pizzas later, we have thousands of memories of friends and family, of sun-drenched lunches and dinners under starry skies.

I've made the most out of the *forno* as I discovered how wonderful wood-fired cooking can be. It takes more than two hours to bring it up to the proper temperature for pizza, and the stone floor and domed ceiling stay hot for more than twelve hours after the last piece of olive wood is thrown on the fire. You can put a pork shoulder, scored and stuffed with garlic slices and rosemary, into the oven at midnight after the pizzas have been consumed, and by noon the next day, the meat is so tender it falls off the bone. Some of our other favorite *forno* recipes are veal shanks with prunes in red wine; chicken *cacciatore*; roasted potatoes in cream with *pancetta* and sage; and peaches bought that morning from the local farmers, grilled in the *forno* and topped with *Vin Santo* and crème fraiche. My passion for cooking, and the compliments I receive after a dinner party, have been one of the few things that have soothed my damaged ego these past ten years, as thoughts of the financial mess that I created with Anderò are never far from my mind.

I treasure my Italian friendships with Nicola and Vittorio, and I'm proud of what we have accomplished at il Borghetto. I still envision a positive outcome for the beautiful la Porcellaia project. I dream of building the three homes with private pools that we have designed for this spectacular Arsina hillside, and I know that I cannot give up now.

Building Dreams in Tuscany. I continue to search for the happy ending.

Epilogue

We have been in la Casa Gialla for thirteen years now. At more than a few of those dinner parties, when the moon rises above the Apennines just after dark, I think I am living a dream. Laughing with friends under the stars at midnight on a warm summer night feels perfect. This is the *bella Toscana* that is so lovely, so enticing, that we were willing to leave our favorite city in the world, London, to come live here. We are surviving as best we can the financial disaster that is Anderò. All the pain of that experience doesn't erase the joy of living *la dolce vita*.

One summer evening, with friends from Chicago dining with us under the pergola, with light in the sky until almost ten o'clock, we were treated to the full moon rising above the Apennine mountains directly to the east of us. "I'm going for my camera and tripod!" shouted my friend. With the lights twinkling far out into the valley, sipping *Limoncello* and *Vin Santo* under the full moon, I thought to myself, "This is why we're here. This is heaven. This is Tuscany."

Jim Kachenmeister